"Hypnotically written and impr... *My Morningless Mornings* is an intense and harrowing meditation on Stefany Anne Golberg's youthful insomnia. More than that, though, it's a moving mini-portrait of the bond between a father and his daughter. I really loved this book."

—**Tom Bissell, author of *Apostle* and co-author of *The Disaster Artist***

"*My Morningless Mornings* is a brilliant book, an exploratory meditation on the significance of day and night, waking and sleeping, light and shadow. It moves fluidly from one object of contemplation to another, giving each a gentle, deft attention that makes it at once familiar and strange. This is a book that works on the reader's mind so that after you finish it, the world around you seems changed, revealed to be more mysterious, fascinating, illuminated and alive than you had realized before."

— **Emily Mitchell, author of *The Last Summer of the World* and *Viral: Stories***

"This extraordinary little book is a cabinet of wonders. Golberg's quest to understand her relationship with the night and her insomnia takes her outward and inward simultaneously, from the deepest realms of her personal history to her brilliant notes on literature, art, and film. Like Patti Smith's *Woolgathering*, Golberg's *My Morningless Mornings* transforms seeming mundanities into magic by viewing life through an artful lens that makes everything feel novel. Pure alchemy."

— **J. M. Tyree, co-author of *Our Secret Life in the Movies***

"It is disorienting to be a stranger. Stefany Anne Golberg's *My Morningless Mornings* takes the memoir beyond facile lyric self-regard and renders the troubling experience of the self as stranger... in childhood, of which we remain tributaries, another world perhaps definitively lost to the recuperation of grieving. This work shows us what it means that writing is re-living."

— Michael Stone-Richards, founding editor, *Detroit Research*

"Golberg brings her razor intellect, eclectic reading, and vast imagination to bear. Are we awake, or are we asleep? Did we dream this book, or did we dream us? Is this the most haunting thought on earth—or the most hopeful?: 'We wake in the morning with the sense that there's something we're supposed to do, but this something has no name.'"

— Heather King, author of *Parched, Shirt of Flame*, and *Ravished.*

"There aren't many things we can isolate as characteristic of all human beings everywhere. Walking on two feet? Wearing clothes? Sleeping by night and going about by day? We will have to scrap the last of these, as Stefany Anne Golberg's stunning work reveals to us the profound humanity of someone who stays up all night, who does not welcome the morning as the beginning of a new day full of promise, but rather experiences it as the dreaded end of that part of her life that is most real, most vital, and sharpest: the night."

—Justin E.H. Smith

my morningless mornings

stefany anne golberg

The Unnamed Press
Los Angeles, CA

ISBN: 9781951213046
eISBN: 9781951213053
Library of Congress Control Number: 2019956870

This book is a work of nonfiction.

Designed and Typeset by Jaya Nicely
Manufactured in the United States of America by Versa Press, Inc.

Distributed by Publishers Group West

First Edition

for Morgan

Wake! The sky is light!

Let us to the road again....

—Basho

my morningless mornings

*I*t's disorienting to wake up in a stranger's house. No matter how welcoming the home—the clean towels laid carefully by the sink, the extra blanket in the drawer—when you wake up in a bed that's not your own, when the sun comes through the window at an unfamiliar slant, when morning feet outside the door sound earlier or later than you expect, and when the objects you so deliberately put around your bed as talismans, that connect you back to the material world you left behind in dreams—dreams of a past in which you never lived, of places you never visited, with people who are odd composites of those you are closest to, like creatures you might see on a shelf in the wonder cabinet of Holy Roman Emperor Rudolf II: fish with unicorn horns, horses with fins, mothers with the heads of fathers, bodies of friends long absent who think like you, children you never birthed who are also somehow yours, dead become living and living become dead, the people of your life become monsters who share limbs and intentions that just don't fit—when those things that are your touchstones to reality go missing, the first moments of waking are hard. Sometimes, when traveling, the places in which you wake will change so often you can stop believing in morning altogether: a motel room in Waycross, Georgia; a bedroom in a parent's house that once belonged to you. Morning becomes dislocated from anything familiar, then. All you can rely on is waking itself and the most basic feature of morning: light coming from darkness.

Have you had many mornings like this, hotel rooms in turnpike towns whose names you would never remember, on couches, on floors, next to cars in the woods? Have you ever had mornings in a bed that was yours but didn't seem to be? On mornings like this, in the stranger's house that may very well be your own, you can't hide from morning's troubles. The cracks in the walls are exposed.

night

*Y*ears ago, when I was fourteen, my father, a professor at the local university, left his teaching position for an indefinite period of absence. He had been experiencing a certain restlessness, and this became anxiety and eventually terror. My father began to spend hours pacing the hallway, sometimes howling angry words, against us, against the enemies inside and out. His usual careless scholar's look became haggard, and he had difficulty sleeping at night. At first, the household tried to proceed as usual. We were so different from one another, but the fear seemed to bind us together. Soon, the fear grew. My brother, who had just turned eighteen, left for college that year and would never return. My mother was preoccupied with tending to my father, until she no longer could and left too. But I had become convinced that to live elsewhere would be unimaginable and that, moreover, my father, left alone, would die.

It was around this time, beginning in late winter I think, that I tried to erase the morning. Morning's burdens could pass me by while I stayed hidden inside. I had stopped going to school and stopped speaking too. I spent my days reading or sleeping—I don't remember exactly how I passed the time, but I lived this way for a month. There was no plan; I was too young to understand plans. I can tell you only that the repetition of lived days had become suddenly and totally unbearable, the reiteration of routine, the forced relationships, the questions and the failure of adults to answer them. At the end of my month of silence, I knew that I would not return to school.

To erase the morning, I had to stretch the night. I stayed awake into the early a.m., until just before sunrise, when I allowed myself to sleep. I slept for a few hours and woke at noon, and, in this way, when I opened my eyes, I was immediately in the p.m. hours, the time most people think of as "day," the efficient, practical, useful hours. The p.m. hours are the worldly hours, but when I was a teenager, the time between roughly 10:00 p.m. and 6:00 a.m. became my true day. I felt most awake at that time. The yard behind my house in Las Vegas and the desert beyond were more vivid than in the busy light of day. If you've seen the desert at night then you know that this is true. The desert, so blinding under the sun, is, when lit up by stars and moon, easier to see. Stars lighted the yard behind my house, and I was lit by the television screen that flickered as long as the stars did. Between 10:00 and 6:00 I kept myself in a state of sleeplessness, not to uncover the mystery of night's puzzles, but to find out what really happens in the liminal space that is the passage from night to day. I was nighttime's watcher.

In the sprawling ranch house ten minutes from the Las Vegas Strip that I had lived in all my life, with its wall-to-wall chocolate-brown carpet and long hallway, I finished my dinner and put my dishes in the sink. We were often together, my father and I, bounded by the walls of the house, but there was an uncrossable sea between us. My father was a mathematician; he would lie on the couch in the day surrounded by papers, working out equations for many years after he'd left the university. Numbers seemed to be the only thing that calmed him. I remember us eating separately, though this had not always been the case.

At 9:00 p.m., my father went to his bedroom. At 10:00 p.m., I sat in the fat tan recliner and turned the TV on. The television played continuously at a low volume; it was the only light in the house. This room, the family room, had become, by that time, the emptiest room of all. I kept a stack of library books beside me on a wooden tray, along with a multivolume encyclopedia containing illustrations of countries that no longer existed, my third edition of *Roget's International Thesaurus*, and a notebook. Because I was completing my diploma via correspondence courses that were mailed from the University of Lincoln–Nebraska to my house, a good number of my daytime hours were spent in the libraries of Las Vegas, lingering especially in the sections where the heavy art books were kept. The company of this man-made beauty, stacked high and low around me, gave my young life a lofty, transported quality. In later years this led to my wandering barely visited rooms in the museums of New York City, or around a city's lesser streets, or driving without purpose through American towns. For the next eight hours the television ran through its cycle of reruns and commercials. Most of the programs played at these hours were well past their due dates: variety shows with performers I'd never heard of and sitcoms with anachronistic jokes, movies with flickering dust particles and dancing and singing, movies I should not have been watching, and many, many documentaries. Early a.m. television was a rest home for lost, rejected culture. I watched these shows intently. I watched the actors' facial gestures and learned bygone references. I learned the old songs and dances. I learned about long-standing resentments and wars. My mind in these hours was porous and calm. I was rarely interrupted.

If I thought I heard my father from his room down the hall, I would mute the sound on the television until I was sure he had gone back to bed. If my father knew I was awake all those nights, he never said. But there were plenty of weeks he wasn't there, and I was in the house alone. Looking back, it seems impossible to me that I could have been awake for so long, every night for years. But time then, as I remember it, never passed slowly.

✳

In the early years of the twentieth century, the philosopher Evelyn Underhill wrote a book called *The Grey World*. It is about a little boy who dies. In the underworld, the boy confronts an over-arching grey. He sees the living world through this grey veil—people are grey, things are grey, everything is grey. Yet the boy is not meant to die and comes back from the world of the dead. Nonetheless, the world of the living, for the boy, remains grey. In one scene, the boy, standing at a window in his new home, looks out on a suburban street between the slats of the closed venetian blinds. The indifference of the houses there seems monstrous to him. In trying to shake free from the overwhelming power of the grey world, the boy has the sudden and alarming impression that the living world is mostly dead and that life is a rare and confusing accident. In the dark hours of predawn, I, too, imagined that the whole city was dead except for me. The world was dead and life, my life, was a rare and confusing accident that could only be met in solitude.

I was especially drawn to the dead artists I read about and saw on TV, because they seemed to be part of a tale that went on and on. Only the dead know the whole story. It's the dead who sleep with me and get up with me in the morning. Rainer Maria Rilke asked, what if the dead don't need us like we need them? But I say, how could they not? We are how the story continues. We are how the dead dream.

At a dinner one evening, at my mother's house in Las Vegas, years after I had left the city and then returned for a visit, a family friend who belonged to a Jewish burial society told me of a body he had recently attended. In Jewish tradition, a dead body must be cared for. It can't just be discarded in a morgue. It must be cleaned and dressed and cannot be left alone for even a second, not even at night, not even if you want to sleep. Someone must take on the task of watching over the dead. They must watch over the dead and say blessings for them until the dead can be buried the next day, because the soul of a person who has just died is in turmoil, and its body is a foreclosed home. In Jewish law, a person who has died and is not yet buried is like a crying newborn. Just as babies need solace until they can get used to their new state of being, so the dead need comfort too. Babies are souls trying to fit into their bodies; the dead are souls who no longer have the comfort of the bodies they spent a lifetime getting used to.

This family friend told me that he and the members of his burial society were strangers to the dead they tended. Their job was to bear the responsibility of keeping the dead person safe so that the family of the dead could grieve. At some point between dinner and dessert, the family friend described to me how, the night before, he and his burial society cleaned the body of a man they had never met when the man was alive. They poured water over him, from head to toe, a long stream of flowing water, and wrapped the dead man's body in a shroud. Then, in the hours between midnight and sunrise, the society took turns watching. *How grateful I was,* said the family friend, *when it was my turn to stand over the stranger, to stand by him and sing for him a cycle of psalms,* singing for a man he did not know and who would never be able to thank him.

A lot of years have passed since I experienced my morningless mornings. But I've since realized that I, too, was keeping vigil back then. The space between night and day is the time for waking and also the time for watching. In the house on University Circle, as my father slept, I kept a sort of vigil, a vigil over a stranger.

✳

How many stories there are about shadows trying to get back to their origins, about people trying to ditch their shadows, about shadows getting deliberately lost from their people, putting on fancy clothes just to spite, dominate, and eventually become people too. You've read these stories. Under the hot light of the desert morning, my shadow and my self felt separated. I could see my shadow well in the morning, spreading out from my feet, but I didn't feel it belonged to me. I carried this shadow around as the day went on—this flimsy, stretched-out reflection. You can't get rid of your shadow in such a light, and you can't get to know it either. At the peak of day, the sun would be so high it would blot out my shadow completely. But in the dark, the shadow and I were together. I couldn't see it but I knew it was there. I didn't have to worry about it dominating me and stealing my clothes and taking over my life. Perhaps, at night, inside, I was mostly shadow. I didn't yet understand this shadow self but I could feel it.

Sleeplessness was my great discovery, darkness my perfect world. As such, I took a keen interest in Jacques Cousteau and his underwater encroachments. In one episode of *The Undersea World of Jacques Cousteau*, Cousteau called the deep ocean "a world without sun." The ocean is a world within the world that seems specially fortified against us. It is fathomless, like hell, and reigns over most of the earth. For me, the undersea world was all the more alluring for being so present and yet so far away. To live in the desert is to dream of water. In the desert, you can't go down. What lies at the desert's depths? You would not want to know.

I especially liked the part in some episodes when the Cousteau team members piled into their self-contained pods—turtles of glass and steel—and cast themselves into the sea. You could never be sure whether the pods would hold or what would be down there, down in the sunless realm. Jacques Cousteau adored Jules Verne. I'd read that Cousteau was a sickly, bedridden child who was never lonely because of his books, so that he would take adventures in his head. You could say that Jacques Cousteau's whole life was a realization of the books he read as a child. In his essay about Jules Verne, Roland Barthes discusses Verne's fascination with ships. Did Verne, who was born on an artificial island in the middle of a river, imagine the island of his childhood unmooring itself from France and floating off and away? Verne wrote many adventures but hardly adventured himself. Any time he had a chance for daring, life got in his way. There is a possibly true story about Verne's first foiled attempt at adventure, which was naturally his most formative, in which an eleven-year-old Verne signs up to be a cabin boy on a three-masted ship headed for the West Indies where, Verne had decided, he would find a coral necklace for his sister. Only young Verne's father caught on to the plan and went to the ship where Verne was stowed, on the eve of what would have been Verne's first adventure, and grabbed his son back to shore, and made the boy promise to travel forevermore "only in his imagination." Verne did buy himself a sailboat in his late thirties, I've read, after he had become successful enough to buy boats. Verne took the little wooden skiff, baptized *Saint-Michel*, along the English coast, and when the *Saint-Michel* became too worn for his taste it was replaced, subsequently, by the *Saint-Michel II* and then the *Saint-Michel III*, the last of which Verne took on his longest voyage, a grand tour around Europe, each new boat mirroring the increasing wealth and fame of the adventure-writer Jules Verne.

Verne's writing is filled with many iterations of ships. Sometimes the ships are submarines, sometimes they are balloons, and sometimes they are boats, but travel, in a Jules Verne story, invariably happens in some sort of vehicle, and that vehicle is usually amazing. Yet even though ships are symbols of departure, wrote Barthes, there is something more to ships than sailing. We may find our love of ships compatible with the romantic, "venturesome" part of our selves, but at a deeper level, a ship is a house; it is an emblem of enclosure. *An inclination for ships*, wrote Roland Barthes, *always means the joy of perfectly enclosing oneself, of having at hand the greatest possible number of objects, and having at one's disposal an absolutely finite space*. People who like ships actually like homes, because a ship is a fully contained habitat. Like a human body, a ship is a blissful, finite cell from which one can safely gaze out upon the unfathomable. A ship is a symbol for the perfection of one's inner humanity.

Sitting in the fat chair with my books and things around me, the last television program would end just as the morning sun came up over the fence and into the yard and through the sliding glass door. Then I could go to my room and get in bed and close my eyes before the morning turned real.

✦

There was a morning, some time ago, when you and I were walking, my love. It was spring and plants were nudging into view. On the ground, I saw a horn. A short, discarded antler. Here it was, spring, with everything growing up and out, and this bit had fallen off. The base of the antler had a soft ring of skin. The ground is filled with bones, you know. Once you start looking you will see them everywhere. That morning, we guessed that we must have missed the young deer by only a few minutes when we had been at the bottom of the hill. I pictured the deer dashing across the meadow with only one antler attached. The antler wasn't heavy, exactly, but weighty. We continued in silence and you said, *There is something significant about discovering dead bones, but this is a bone of the living.*

Along the highway, above the hill, the cars raced by. I don't think these people realized they were passing by a graveyard. But then every place on Earth is a graveyard. In America, we've made special parks to separate the places of the dead from the places of the living. But we all know that graveyards are a ruse, that there are no special places where we can live apart from the dead. Even our bodies, it must be said, are graveyards.

Years ago, just after the fall of the Communist regime, I went to the Sedlec Ossuary outside Prague. The bones of the Czech dead were collected and stacked and displayed for all to see. The display made me instantly uncomfortable, not because the ossuary was gruesome, but because it was so intimate. I did not know what to do in the presence of this naked orgy of bones. I was struck, too, by grief so boldly exhibited. Death, to me, was meant to be hidden, just as bones are hidden by flesh. I knew, then, why so many shamans and ancient people believed that the soul resides in the bones. Bones are the balance between the seen and unseen, between perception and concealment, revealed in death but secret in life. You could say that morning is like bones too, like a woman who takes off her skirt and uses it to hide her face.

In the end, we can know so little of morning. Whatever we do learn, I think, takes a lifetime.

✦

In paintings, morning looks like renewal; it is fresh and beautiful like spring. In paintings, afternoon is adulthood, dusk is middle age, and nighttime is the end. But morning, in paintings, is little children.

✦

In the evenings, I started making visits to my backyard. No one had stepped foot in the yard for years and it had grown over with desert scrub. Guests no longer came to our house, and no one had the energy to care for the yard and force it to be more welcoming. Lounging in a desert yard is a challenge. The desert does not invite us to lounge. The prophets would tell you that spending long periods in the desert is only for those who yearn to be close to death. Americans especially dislike death, but dislike even more being told where they should be, and many residents of my hometown attempted all sorts of methods to spite the desert's dominion, just so they might triumphantly and defiantly lounge. Some Las Vegas residents drove spectacular holes into the sand and filled the holes with bright blue water, and they would stay submerged for hours, barely shielded from the bald solar rays. When I was a child, a stiff, drought-resistant grass was introduced to the city and quickly spread across suburbia. It was a grass impossible to walk on, but it thrived in the heat, and some people called it "devil's-grass." Caring for this grass that survived on scarcity, that needed so little from people and, indeed, crowded out every other living thing in its path, was more like being a grave attendant than a gardener. In subsequent years, on weekends, you would see rows and rows of Las Vegas residents standing in their driveways, spraying waves of pesticide around lawn chairs that were never used. I have a vague memory of my mother, from the time we all lived together, tending roses along the cinder block fence that separated our house from the neighbors'. Without regular care or the will to destroy it, the grass that had been planted over the sand behind my house when I was born was long and yellow by my teenage years. Eventually, the yard became neither sand nor lawn. The grass refused to recede and so the desert could not be, and nothing else was invited to grow there.

With the television still going inside, I sat for hours on the concrete patio and watched the stars. The desert sky is a tremendous sight because it is never truly dark. In America's East or in the South, a hot night will ring with the singing and trilling of creatures—the crickets, the frogs, the nocturnal birds—but the desert at night is still. Many holy seekers have left civilization and gone to the desert to stuff their ears with silence. But even they can't escape the desert's sidereal celebration. Long after midnight, the stars cast their glow on my backyard and, in the distance, on the mountains that lined the city, turning everything to silhouette. The mountains lay flat on the horizon, flat as all substance flattens in the desert—eternal, ungraspable flatness. And in the space between the top of the world and the mountains was another glow: the Las Vegas Strip, with its ten thousand radiant bulbs. It's funny. You could be on the Strip and hear only the Strip, be engulfed by the Dionysian roar of casino life, the barker's call in the windowless den, the heel on the stage, coin against coin, will against will, the pageantry and the ecstasy of forgetting. Fifteen minutes away, in a yard behind a house, the Strip would be mute but the lights still shining. It was like watching a party scene in a silent film or an explosion miles away. The builders of the Strip constructed their very own galaxy. This was Edison's vision come to pass—Thomas Edison, our Menlo Park Prometheus, who foiled the gods with lightbulbs and achieved the astonishing feat of bringing starlight to Earth. Lightbulbs would give us a power over the night. They would give people everlasting day. This is a beautiful wish. But what Edison did not consider was that to kill darkness one must also kill light. Lightbulbs complicated the natural balance between light and dark. They generated a no-time where night and day were collapsed. In the cave of the casino, lightbulbs cancel both darkness and daylight and create, in essence, a sensation of timelessness.

I have an uneasy relationship with artificial light. Lamps in my home are set in odd places where they train light into corners, or on the floor, or random spots on the ceiling, and any indoor space under my charge is more likely to invite shadows than light, which is why, even though I found the sun so oppressive when I was young, as I've aged I've become more attracted to interior spaces with breezy windows that let the sun shoot in and light up the room. Big windows let me delight in the sunshine and, more than that, release me from the trouble of auto-illumination. Not that bulbs are without their charms. Recently, I visited the studio of a light artist in Cleveland, where I was introduced to the magical properties of fluorescent tubes, how different gases make their own color, and how light and color can be reanimated in a bulb that has lain dormant for years. Strewn around this artist's studio were salvaged beer signs waiting for resurrection. On a table was a row of heavy black generators and enchanted wands the artist used to shock the light back into being. This artist was a Dr. Frankenstein of neon. Never before had I truly appreciated the magnificence of artificial lighting, the subtleties of gas, how argon and krypton and xenon, when brought under glass like terrariums, can create different hues and affect the way we experience space and time. When I asked the man why he had chosen to be an artist of light, he spoke of all the bulbs that he had saved over the decades and the people who helped him, who would bring him old bulbs from vacant buildings around Cleveland or signs from restaurants that had closed, and I understood that what attracted this artist most to his medium was not so much the aesthetics of fake lighting, but the joy of saving light. Whereas the sun does not seem to need us at all, a lightbulb can't shine without the help of a person. Every time we switch on a light, we can be participants in a tiny Genesis; all the shadows go running. The novelist Jun'ichirō Tanizaki put it very well when he wrote, *Light is used not for reading or writing or sewing but for dispelling the shadows in the farthest corners.*

Tanizaki, who is known for his 1933 essay titled "In Praise of Shadows," in which he discusses what was then called the "Eastern" appreciation of shadows, in contrast to what was then called the "Western" love of light, which was demonstrated not just in Westerners' fondness for artificial bulbs and electricity, but also in their love of bright, shiny surfaces: polished silver, sparkling diamonds, glass. But in tarnished tin and muddy jade and candlelight, explained Tanizaki, one lives in harmony with shadows that are, incidentally, the keepers of the Eastern past. This "sheen of antiquity," wrote Tanizaki, is really just dirt, the poetry of grime. Tanizaki tells a story in his essay about visiting a restaurant in Kyoto, the Waranjiya. A main attraction of the Waranjiya, he explained, was its candlelit dining rooms. But when he arrived one spring after a long leave, all the candles had been replaced by electric lamps in the style of old-fashioned lanterns. Tanizaki, who was born in the nineteenth century but matured in the twentieth, was told by the staff that the change had taken place after several customers complained that the candlelight was too dim. However, the staff of the Waranjiya was happy to bring Tanizaki a candle stand for his table. Tanizaki accepted. By the flickering of this candle stand in the small, square room of the Waranjiya, the novelist Jun'ichirō Tanizaki gazed into his dinner plate. He saw in this plate not the brilliant shimmer of the ocean in summer, like you might see in a crystal goblet on a table someplace in Toledo, but rather the beauty of a still, dark pond.

What allowed Tanizaki to see the beauty of shadows was that he allowed himself to look. I'm certain this is why Tanizaki began his essay with a short discourse on hiding. What a great effort it is, wrote Tanizaki, to build a house in pure Japanese style, *striving somehow to make electric wires, gas pipes, and water lines harmonize with the austerity of Japanese rooms ... The purist may rack his brain over the placement of a single telephone, hiding it behind the staircase or in a corner of the hallway .... He may bury the wires rather than hang them in the garden, hide the switches in a closet or cupboard, run the cords behind a folding screen. Yet for all his ingenuity, his efforts often impress us as nervous, fussy, excessively contrived.* Beauty, wrote Tanizaki later in his essay, *must always grow from the realities of life.* The more we struggle to conceal our electric cords behind rice paper screens, the more they demand to be known. *Seen at dusk,* wrote Jun'ichirō Tanizaki, *as one gazes out upon the countryside from the window of a train, the lonely light of a bulb under an old-fashioned shade, shining dimly from behind the white paper shoji of a thatch-roofed farmhouse, can seem positively elegant.*

There's a painting by an Englishman, Sir Luke Fildes, that makes me think of what the Waranjiya might have looked like that night Tanizaki arrived after a long time away, staring into his dinner plate by the light of a candle; what the Waranjiya might have looked like if it were a home instead of a restaurant, if it were a place of mourning rather than fine dining. Fildes's painting is of a room—a dim, low-ceilinged room. The room is stocked with props and there are four characters in the scene. Fildes painted two sources of light in this room, a window and a lamp under an old-fashioned shade. The room is mostly dark, but the faint light coming from the lamp and the window has created a lodging for shadows. Child-sized nightgowns hang on a line along the ceiling's wooden beams. There's a bowl and spoon untouched on the bench and, next to them, a white pitcher. At the center of Fildes's painting is a boy laid out across two kitchen chairs. Next to the boy, on another chair, is a doctor. The boy lies helpless on his makeshift bed, but the doctor, seated between the bed and a sick table, one hand on his thigh and the other propping his chin, looks even more helpless. The doctor has clearly reached the limits of care; he can only contemplate the patient. The doctor, no longer a healer, has been reduced to watching. Nonetheless, you can see from his posture and the squint of his eyes that the doctor is still thinking, still trying to match puzzle pieces, trying with the fullest power of his mind to will some anima into the boy's limp body.

The shade on the lamp by the doctor is bent all the way to the right, so that there is no protecting the doctor from the bare light. Lamps can be selective in what they choose to show. For every person brightened another becomes hidden. I think Fildes must have cocked the lampshade the way he did to maximize his theme of human impotence. With the shade pulled sharply to the right, the lamp beams its verdict upon the doctor and the boy and their teacup of medicine on the nightstand. The lamp makes the row of nightgowns recede into the wall. The hanging family portrait is dim; the door scarcely exists. You can just make out the boy's parents in the background, the father's hand on the mother's shoulder, his body turned away from hers. The father is watching the doctor. His grief is protected from the lampshade's aim.

But on the right side of the painting, next to the parents and across from the lamp, a trace of morning light is coming through the window. It spills over the mother, slumped on the table, onto the flowerpot someone must have put on the sill days earlier. The morning light hardly reaches the father, and it ignores the doctor altogether. And then there is the boy. The figure of the boy lies between the lamp of night shining on his front and the glow of dawn behind, drawing him away from the room. The light of dawn just touches the hair of the boy. As the two light sources meet around the boy's head, they make a little halo.

Ever since Fildes exhibited *The Doctor* in 1891, people have argued over the true subject of the painting. Is it about the painter's own son, Philip, who died when he was one year old? Is it the parents and their despair, or is the subject, as the title instructs, the doctor himself? When I look at *The Doctor* I see a painting of the never-ending anxiety of morning. The glass lamp is the stolen light of Prometheus, the light of reason and Edison and willpower and casinos. The window is the light that belongs to the gods. It is the light we can't control and can't steal. The glass lamp wants to push away the morning light, to keep the reason of nighttime going as long as it can. It wants to deny the change, whether it's hopeful or not. It wants to burn death out of the picture. It wants to refuse the morning. The doctor, in his lamp-side vigil, is holding on to the night, certain he can find the answers. The father, between the two lights, keeps suspended in time for as long as he can. But by the light of dawn, the mother, the boy, and the flowerpot are forced into tomorrow.

＊

As it happens, I've read Thomas Edison hardly ever slept at night.

＊

There are two times in the day our shadows are longest: when the sun rises and when the sun sets. At these times, the sun is closest to us. Is it a coincidence that the shadow is so long in the morning? The sun moves away from us and up into the sky, and the shadow becomes small and forgettable. It rests over our heads like a hat, close to our heads but far from our eyes. Then, at night, the shadow comes back. It returns to its place alongside us and grows and grows until it saturates the atmosphere, until everything is shadow.

3:00 AM

When I was very young, when my parents and brother still slept in their rooms down the hall, the monsters came in flames. It was 3:00 a.m. or thereabouts, always the same hour, always the same state. Three a.m. was morning, but light felt so far. I don't think there is another time when daylight feels so distant. At 3:00 a.m. I could hear the sound of air breaking inside the walls. I could see behind closed eyes my house filled with fire. At 3:00 a.m. I would plan my escape route; I had planned this many times before. I would leave through the window, though it had never been opened and would never be as long as I slept there. But when my house caught on fire, as I knew it would one day, then through the window I would go. Only, in my mind, I could never go, because I first had to decide which of my things would come with me. In my bed, at the terrible hour, I was paralyzed with fear for my things. The objects in my room were everything to me; to imagine them burning filled me with panic. So I would mentally scan my room for emblems, for the things that best represented my things, my beautiful things that were about to be consumed in what I was sure would be the famous fire of University Circle. I could not fall asleep, could not permit myself to fall asleep, until the decisions were made. For an hour or more, I would assess my relationship to each of my belongings, each memento, each toy, measuring its emotional weight on a cosmic scale with me on one end and the thing on the other, to see who balanced whom. Then, at long last, I would make my decision. I could sleep then, an hour or so, until my mother woke me and sent me off to school. A week later, there I would be at 3:00 a.m., listening to the creaking in the walls and going through the unbearable process all over again.

As I grew older, the terrible hour became more inchoate, more unreal. The voices in my head did not seem to belong to me, and what they told me I cannot repeat. Perhaps you already know. In a Brooklyn apartment, sometime in my thirties, I watched an Ingmar Bergman film that began: *Johan Borg disappeared without a trace from his home on the island of Baltrum in the Frisian Islands*. In that film, I finally learned the name of 3:00 a.m. This is the worst hour, Johan tells his wife Alma, as they sit at the kitchen table in the dark. *Do you know what it's called?* Johan says. *No*, she says, and he says, *The old people used to call it the "Hour of the Wolf." It's the hour at which most people die and most children are born. It's now that the nightmares come to us. And if we are awake...* says Johan, lighting matches and watching them burn. The Hour of the Wolf is the hour of meat eaters, of insects, and of spider men. It is the hour of the schoolmaster, the old lady threatening to take off her hat, and all the cast-iron, cackling women.

I've read that 3:00 in the morning is the time when most crimes are committed and when most fevers either break or triumph. No one knows why, but people who work in hospitals will tell you that 3:00 in the morning is a critical hour for the dying. At Wolf Time, I've read, the dead become suddenly awake. The demons reveal themselves. *Inter canem et lupum*, the medievals called it, the time between the dog and the wolf. At Wolf Time the dog seeks his rest and the wolf seeks out his prey. There's no other way to say this: Wolf Time is the devil's time. The Hour of the Wolf is the nightmare that can't be slept through. Have you ever had a nightmare like this? You can't sleep and you don't know if you are awake. You want to move but can't. You can't open your eyes and you're not dreaming. It is a state between dreaming and waking. At this hour your thoughts are not your own; you don't want them to belong to you. They whisper to you that nothing is real, that your path is false, that you don't know who you are. You are not in control of your thoughts, and the more you clutch at truth the more it turns against you. At 3:00 in the morning you are abandoned. You know that you have failed. 3:00 in the morning is the hour of Judgment; maybe this is how it will be in the moments just after death. Maybe you are dead. And yet how could it be that your life is over and you are still alive? At 3:00 in the morning the metaphors fall away; what remains is the stark fact of nothingness. Daylight is the glue that holds belief together. In the early hours of morning, at the Hour of the Wolf, belief goes to pieces. You might will yourself to get up at 3:00 a.m. in order to break the spell. But the more conscious you are at 3:00 in the morning the less consciousness is yours. At the Hour of the Wolf, you become lost in your own bed. Retracing the steps back to yourself only takes you further away. The house is haunted because you are.

When I was young, my mother assured me that there were no wolves to fear, that the reign of the wolves had ended, that the wolves had been killed long ago to make way for the ways of people. But later, when I was old enough to learn for myself, I read that wolves were still very much around. Wolves, as I understood it, almost always preyed on children. Children are slower, of course, and weaker, but also prone to wandering in places where adults do not dare to go and more likely to greet wolves as friends. When wolves attacked adults, the adults were usually women. I supposed women were attacked by wolves when they went searching for their children or when they wandered off themselves. Wandering leads to wolves. The wolf is therefore an archetype of wandering. The wolf is neither here nor there. As the wolves are caught between human and animal, so are we caught between wolf and self.

Inter canem et lupum. The dog is our tamed, gentle, enlightened side. Our wolf part is savagery and unreason. The primitive wolf self inside us that anthropologist Loren Eiseley wrote about, the part of us that once dwelled with the wolves in uneasy peace, is still there, hidden inside our cloak. Eiseley was writing in winter when this thought came to him. It was night and the wind shook the windows. There was Loren Eiseley, working in his study with a dog asleep at his feet. On his desk was the fossilized leg bone of a bison under a circle of lamplight. The hour was around midnight. All of a sudden, he heard a heavy rasping and the sound of bone on bone. Eiseley's dog had snatched the old leg off the desk and now held it in his jaws. The dog had a wrath in his eyes that Eiseley did not recognize. He began to growl at Eiseley and would not return the bone. The dog's eyes said, I love you, but we are in another time now. *I will not give it up, I cannot. The shadows will not permit me.* With the bone in the dog's mouth, the ancient past, wrote Eiseley, was fully alive inside him. Eiseley withdrew his hand from the growling dog and stood watching. The dog, seeing that Eiseley had backed off, dropped the bone to the floor but set his paw on top of it. Eiseley then suggested to his dog that they go for a walk in the snow. At this proposal, Eiseley's dog, whose name happened to be Wolf, became a pet once more. The two ranged in the cold for a while, and when they returned, Wolf went back to the cozy fire. He was soon asleep and dreaming. *And were there no shadows in my mind?* Eiseley wondered. Hadn't he, the scholar in his study, been ready as well to pounce upon a ten-thousand-year-old bone? *Even to me,* wrote Loren Eiseley, *the shadows had whispered.* It's a disquieting idea that Eiseley poses. We are still hunted by wolves.

When you look at medieval paintings of wolves, you might notice a recurring theme of people stripping off their clothes. Clothes are a symbol of civilization. They are a fortress against the elements, those without and those within. Pliny the Elder tells a story in his *Natural History* about a ritual performed by the Arcadians. Every so often, wrote Pliny, a male family member of the Arcadians would be selected by lottery and taken to a lake. There, the elect would take off his clothes and hang them on a nearby oak tree. Naked, the man would wade into the lake and start to swim across. At the other shore he entered into the forest and there became a wolf. For nine years he lived among them. This man had to keep himself away from other human beings during his wolf years because he would be unable to resist attacking them. Nine years passed in this way. At the end of the last year, if he had succumbed wholly to the ways of the wolves and did not try to escape, the man could return to the Arcadians. At that time, he would go back once more to the lake. He would wade in and swim across, just as he did before, toward his family and friends. At the opposite shore the man would see his clothes hanging on the tree, just as he had left them.

In the old tales, a man sometimes becomes a wolf when he has been attacked by wolves or otherwise cursed. The werewolf then attacks humans and suffers, because he has yielded to the ways of the beast. The way Pliny tells it, Arcadians believed that the best way to hold on to one's humanity was to voluntarily join the wolves for a time.

At the opening of Bergman's film, during the credits, you can hear the sound of hammers. A man says, *Can someone move that chair?* There is laughing, and drilling, and more banging. It's the sound of the movie crew building the set, setting the scene, preparing to tell Alma's story, the way she has told it to the director. A scene later, Bergman puts us back in time, to a day when Johan has not yet disappeared without a trace, and he and Alma are together. Why does Bergman start the film this way, revealing the movie magic? Is it a documentary or fiction? Are we forward in time or backward, or is the story just beginning? There are no answers to these questions, I'm afraid. You might as well ask if madness is artificial or real, if terror happens now or then, if morning and night and all concepts of time are vital or arbitrary.

✳

Last night, when we turned off the lights, I saw moonlight pouring in through the bedroom window and spilling over the sheets, just before closing my eyes. My hand next to you was invisible, but the other hand was drenched in white light. I opened this hand and closed it and turned it over and around and let the moon drip into my fingers. The moon spread over my palm, and I remembered that time you told me why you liked Compline so much, because the prayers don't pretend. Compline doesn't pretend that monsters aren't under the bed, pretend we were wrong as children, pretend that black thoughts in the middle of night will not try their best to consume us. Compline knows what happens when you are left alone with your mind, that at night you are left alone. You had just returned that evening from praying with three elderly nuns and their dog. You chanted in a single room in a mostly forgotten monastery concealed in a crease of New York, between mountains on one side and a sprawling golf club that knocked balls into the monastery pond and made the dog bark in the day. You left that chapel comforted, assured that these nuns had your back and that just by the act of mutual non-pretending the demons would have less of you to work with.

Sometimes, when I picture people writing, I picture them at windows. I wondered, last night, as I lay there beside you holding the moon, if the authors of Compline wrote those prayers just before sleeping, at the beginning of the long and horrible road to morning. I wondered what kinds of windows were near them and how many nights of writing had to pass before prayers seemed like something to try.

✳

Our bodies stay the same when the sun disappears, but where do our shadows go? Do they stop existing or do they retreat to a corner of the house and we just can't see them? In school, we're taught how a shadow is made. We are not told how a shadow lives.

✳

Yesterday morning I woke up without you. In the kitchen, I found a half-crushed ant on the floor. It was writhing in a square of morning light. This is how I saw it. Earlier, someone had stepped on the ant without noticing, accidentally, perhaps when she came to the kitchen for a second cup of coffee, but that person had not entirely crushed it. Exactly how long the ant had been there I didn't know. The ant rubbed its front legs over its bottom half, as if it were trying to smooth out its pain. I sat on the floor beside the ant and tried whispering words of encouragement, but this did not seem to help. I decided the ant would be more comfortable outside than on the cold kitchen floor. I myself hope to die in the fresh summer air under a tree and wished this for the ant, though I worried about moving it too far from its friends, who would recover it, I've read, to be buried among its kind.

Ants are the pallbearers of morning. They move in trails along the floors and windowsills, shouldering the dead. In early morning the funeral procession of ants is long but looks longer in shadow, and the ants' burdens stretch their size too. Once, at sunrise in a far-off country, I watched a moth float over the floor upside down. A tiny ant with a big dead moth on its back is more than an individual ant. It has two bodies then, and two lives as well, a flying life that has ceased flying and a crawling life that staggers and wobbles, buckling under the weight of the corpse it carries. In summertime, the ants move in the orange magic hour of light and their mute procession glows, until eight o'clock comes and the march of ants vanishes into the walls.

With some difficulty, I gathered the ant in my hand and took us both outside. Near a tree, in a shady spot by the mint, I placed the ant slowly down. This was an area of the yard reserved for the dead and dying. A woodpecker rested there, a titmouse, a catbird, a pile of bones. Each had a headstone made from the bark the chestnut tree shed in the fall. The ant kept writhing, not knowing if it wanted to go forward or backward. I went to the kitchen, returned with a pinch of sugar, and sprinkled it by the ant's head.

Ralph Waldo Emerson wrote that the instincts of the ant are very unimportant until we see the ant in relation to us, and then every little habit in the ant's body becomes sublime. He also noted a "recent" scientific observation that ants never sleep. They just rest long enough to go again. Time, for people, is experienced largely through waking and sleep. Without morning, we wouldn't even be people. Ants, on the contrary, who are never truly asleep, get a taste of immortality, and it could be that we who try to shorten our sleep, or wish to cancel it altogether, come close to experiencing time like ants.

✦

Perhaps you've heard the story of Peter Schlemihl, the protagonist of *The Wonderful History of Peter Schlemihl*, by the French exile and German poet Adelbert von Chamisso. Peter Schlemihl, you might know, is the man who sells his shadow to the Devil for an infinitely replenishing bag of gold. It's not good to sell your shadow to the Devil, but Peter Schlemihl is a young man; he knows well the value of gold and not at all the value of his shadow, until he loses it, that is, only then it is too late. Chamisso never explicitly says what the shadow represents. Yet the instant Schlemihl takes his shadowless self into the world, he becomes an outcast among men. In daylight, people notice right away Schlemihl's deficiency. They mock him, run from him, treat him with contempt. Within minutes, Schlemihl realizes his tragedy. *Where has the gentleman left his shadow?* cries the sentinel at the city gate. *Jesus Maria!* yells a group of women, *the poor fellow has no shadow!* Walking down the street with his bag of gold, Schlemihl takes care to avoid the sun. He bolts from one shady place to another, but this is not sustainable. Schlemihl's next idea is to lock himself in a first-class hotel with his gold and never go out in daylight. The lack of shadow drives Schlemihl into darkness. A rich man—the richest man—lonely Schlemihl sits in his armchair buying up articles from visiting tradesmen, trying to rid himself of his gold. He hires a local artist to paint him a false shadow, but the artist declines and advises Schlemihl to keep hiding. That, the artist believes, is the only rational plan. In the company of servants, Schlemihl feels less than the lowest of them, for even the lowest man has a shadow and moves in the sunshine as he pleases.

I heard the name Schlemihl many times growing up. I understood it was a word for someone who did everything wrong, a bungler, a goof, though I later learned that the name is Yiddish and means "one who is denied worldly success." After a year and a day of his shadowless life, Peter Schlemihl meets the Devil once more. The Devil is happy to give Schlemihl back his shadow, along with his reentry into the world of people. In exchange, the Devil wants Schlemihl's soul. This proposal is Schlemihl's last gamble. He has lost all hope of being loved. The townspeople devastated his home and smashed his windows. Every servant has fled. *A rich man like you needs a shadow*, the Devil tells him. But Peter Schlemihl refuses. He has grown sick of his dependency on the Devil, and his sickness becomes his strength. In an instant, Schlemihl decides he will wander forever—no gold, no friends, no love, no aim, no hope, and no shadow. He lurks in the woods. When he comes to a spot where the sun shines through the trees, Schlemihl waits hours for the sun to move, lest some person should see him. Peter Schlemihl is never so attentive to light as after he loses his shadow. (The Hungarian writer Imre Kertész came up with a perfectly apt way of describing the feeling of losing one's shadow in his novel *Liquidation*: an "oppressive sense of implausibility.") In a fantastic twist, to replace his worn-out shoes, Schlemihl unknowingly buys a pair of seven-league boots, the boots of European folktales that allow their wearer to cover great distances in a single step, and with these Schlemihl finds his new fortune: he becomes a globetrotter extraordinaire and an extraordinary naturalist. He sees Egyptian pyramids and the rice paddies of China, the polar glaciers and Sumatra and Cape Horn. He sees the caves of Thebes where Paul the Hermit had dwelled and chooses one for his home. *I fell in speechless adoration on my knees and shed tears of thankfulness ... For early offence thrust out from the society of men, I was cast, for compensation, upon Nature, which I ever loved; the earth was given me as a rich garden, study for the object and strength of my life, and science for its goal.* Living in his cave contented, with his marvelous boots and his natural histories and his poodle, Peter Schlemihl, at last, is free. He cheated the Devil, yet at the cost of cheating himself out of a connection to life. He is still a vampire, running from both darkness and light, enjoying the world without participating in it, unable to share his shadow.

Our modern vampire—the vampire created around Chamisso's time, the nineteenth century—is not the same as vampires of folktales past. Vampires of old were menacing fiends, whereas our vampire is a melancholy hero. The vampires of the past stole blood from the living in order to acquire their life essences. The bloodlust of the present-day vampire is less a compulsion to stay undead (though this is a factor) than an ache to connect with the living. Of course, the two go hand in hand. And while they can't be called eternal, our vampires have an inescapable longing for eternity, and this makes them romantic and tragic. Vampires are people who cannot accept the terms of mortality; they cannot live and are afraid to die. Vampires cast no shadow, much like Peter

Schlemihl, and have a hatred of mirrors too, and anything that reflects them back on themselves. But what most distinguishes today's vampires from those of yesterday is their terrible dread of morning. I've read that vampires of folklore were not unusually bothered by sunlight and could roam as they pleased in the day. But in the modern incarnation of vampires, the loathing of morning is intrinsic. Awake in the dark and to bed before the first ray of dawn—this is the life of the vampire we know. Nothing is more horrible to vampires than sunrise; they are eaten alive by the sun. The morning light races into the hollow veins of the vampire, shoots through their limbs like lightning. In the final scenes of *Nosferatu*, F. W. Murnau's illicit cinematic rendering of Bram Stoker's *Dracula*, the filmmaker shows a row of city structures beyond an open bedroom window. Nosferatu, unprotected and tricked into morning by love, feasts on the neck of the good Ellen. A cock crows. You cannot hear it but Nosferatu does, and so does Knock (Murnau's Renfield) from the corner of his asylum room. Nosferatu turns toward the sound and puts his hand over his heart. Sunlight pours over the buildings but Nosferatu does not run. He staggers to the window, drawn by an internal force. With his left hand still on his heart, the vampire puts his right arm over his eyes, spins toward the sun, and reaches out. Then Nosferatu dissolves into a pitiful wisp of smoke. The vampire life can't be called life, despite its beautiful illusions. It is really suspended animation. A bedroom window in morning reminds vampires of their deathlessness and is a secret wish for annihilation.

When you learn about the childhood of Bram Stoker—how he did not stand upright until the age of seven; how he was considered, by his family and medical professionals, to be in perpetual danger of dying; how he spent his earliest years on the third floor of a house in Clontarf, on the north side of Dublin, watching ships sail in the Dublin Bay—when you learn about the illness from which he suffered, an illness identified, most often, as "unexplained," it's difficult not to find parallels in his writing between the coffin and the bed and, more than that, between exile and sleep. How many nights do we go down and wonder, *Where am I going? Where am I to go? Where am I?* When Count Dracula arrives in London, he brings along fifty boxes of dirt and places them around the city. The boxes are gradually discovered by Dracula's enemies, but their function remains a mystery. At last they learn the truth: Dracula has come from Transylvania intending to settle in London. But he can sleep only in the earth of his native land, or more precisely, the earth in which his ancestors are buried. Dracula must carry his dead with him wherever he goes. He must sleep with the dead but is an alien among them. So Dracula's coffins are not beds for a man who cannot die, as the reader might believe at first. They are portable graves for a man who cannot live. Dracula, it seems, never truly rests and is never really home. Night after night, he plants himself in the soil, a long-expired seed. He can't grow roots to blossom in the sun, and the ground won't take him back.

✳

The poets say that sleep is a rehearsal for death. How you would prove this I don't know, but what the man said to me was this: when we are young our dreams are strong, because we can't stop wanting, not even in sleep. In our dreams, when we are young, we are grasping and falling and flying, just like we are in life. As we age, our dreams start to include memories, and the past feeds the dreams even more. But when we get old—if we get old—dreaming fades away. In time, sleep becomes dreamless, he said, because we are preparing to die. A life can be long but death is longer, and unlike the future of a child, which is busy with hopes for the path ahead, for the old the path is clear. *Have you ever noticed,* he said, his wrinkled hands set one on top of the other, *how the sleep of children is full of nightmares? It's because they are so alive.*

Have you ever feared that you would not see morning? Have you ever roused yourself in the night on purpose, tossed yourself onto the brink of consciousness, just so that you didn't, in falling asleep, accidentally fall dead? At night there are the unspoken questions: *What will I wake into? What world? What room? Which version of myself?* So many repetitions of morning, every one a mystery. How many mornings does it take to know anything at all about morning? Mornings of grey when a sliver of sunlight makes a spot on the wall. Mornings we can still see the moon. Mornings after the first night you yielded your bed to another. Mornings your phone shows twenty missed calls and you know it's finally done. Mornings watching birds leaving nests. Mornings of first snows. Mornings of saying this can never happen again. Mornings of standing afraid before the door. Mornings of the first white hair in the mirror. How many mornings with the windows open and how many with them sealed? How many mornings waking up in a room you won't ever see again? How many mornings to think, *I've lasted another day?* How many mornings until you realize that, wherever you go, there, too, is morning? There are infinite iterations of morning. That morning will be is a given.

The poets say that sleep is a rehearsal for death, that each day dies with sleep, but this is because sleep is the only aspect of death we, the living, can recognize. We fall back on our beds, or the floor, or the ground on a hillside somewhere, and a part of us can pretend. *Ah*, we can say, *I am dying now*.

The vampires know what the poets don't: waking is closer to death than sleep. It's when we wake in the morning and land in unknown territory that we feel we might actually, for a moment, be dead. Arriving in the next day, we have to let the last day go truly, because it won't ever come again.

＊

Science says we dream hardest in morning. Our brains are working at the height of their unreason. It's as though the dreams are trying their best, in these hours, to push themselves before our eyes, so that we will pay attention to them. In the days of morningless mornings, my dreams were very vivid, and I was often confused about what had happened to me in waking life and what was only dream. When you erase mornings, the dream world and the waking world are hard to pull apart, and eventually I started to wonder if the dream world wasn't the waking world or even the other way around. But more than that, my morning dreams made me wonder if these distinctions even made sense. I would find myself staring at the cereal I ate at noon certain I had seen it already in a dream. Sometimes the cereal would appear more real because I was awake. But sometimes the dream world cereal was more real because I had eaten it there first. What would you call this? Verisimilitude, maybe. Reality seemed ever to be trying to prove itself.

Because I assumed my dreams were more vivid than those of others, I decided they must be harbingers of special truths. On the table next to the fat chair I kept library books about dreaming. While I was searching for order in the irrational narratives of my dreams, the books suggested I should instead be probing them for signs.

I started to keep a notepad by my bed. Did I want to make the dreams more or less real by putting words to them? This notepad, I will tell you, has since been lost. But I discovered that, in writing, I mostly dreamed exaggerated variations on mundane conversations I'd had the week before, said words I had wanted to say but didn't, walked into rooms I didn't recognize that were usually rooms in my house, the place I spent most of my time. The banality of my dreams only increased their solidity and importance. I would, occasionally, wake with the belief that I had dreamed an extraordinary dream. One night, I dreamed I was running with a herd of dolphins in an underground parking garage. After the dolphin dream, I started to doubt the insight of the dream world.

I've heard it said that dreaming is like watching a movie of your imagination. This statement, I believe, is meant to imply that we stand outside our dreams, looking in. But dreaming is not like watching. Dreaming happens to us, and even though its substance might be irrational, you can't say that you don't experience a dream. Every little story our minds make up can feel as real as a walk, even if that walk is through the land of dreams.

I often have dreams of falling and they always happen in the morning, always around the same time, just before I wake up. Sometimes I start my day with the feeling that I have just fallen from a great height and landed into my life. Two mornings ago, I dreamed that I was falling, but in this dream I also landed. They used to say that if you fall in your dreams and wake up in the air you will live. But if you hit the ground still dreaming, you are certain to wake up dead.

In the dream, I was not myself but a child. I was with a group of children of various ages; I was an older one. We were on a bench of sorts—a thin wooden board, a platform. It was like the plank that juts from the side of a pirate ship, ready to expel rebellion. This plank, however, did not hang off a ship but the side of an incredible tower, the kind of tower too high for the architects of the waking world. None of the children questioned how our placement on this platform came to pass; we discussed only how to get off. Someone would offer a proposal, but each proposal was met with suspicion, which was then met, inevitably, with silence. The weather up on that plank was cool and plain, almost like the absence of weather. In the midst of one silence, one child slipped. Then a girl made a decision. She was tired of waiting, she told us. She said, *I'm going down*. She did not ask for anyone's approval. She was just suddenly clinging to a silver pipe she claimed ran the length of the tower and led all the way to the ground. The boy next to her wanted to leave too. So they wrapped their arms and legs around each other and down the pipe they inched. This change in the status quo created unease among the rest of us left up on the plank. As the others were shifting and talking, I decided I was getting off too. Only, instead of moving to the pipe with care like the girl, I just stood up all at once. And like that I was standing and felt the full measure of my position hovering over the clear blue void. I leaned over the edge, in slow motion, so slowly I could feel that moment when I believed I could pull myself back. It was then it became clear to me that I was going to fall. *I am going to fall*, I said out loud, and then I was. I had often heard that staying relaxed lessens the impact from a great fall. I guess I did not wake because, in the dream, I did not allow myself to be afraid. Consequently, I crashed to the bottom and remained in my dream. The other children had managed to get safely down in the time that I was falling, and they were waiting for me at the bottom, like Dorothy's family around her bed after she returns home from Oz. The first girl who escaped the plank leaned over to consider me. I said, *We are still living*, and woke.

✳

They say that Early Man once slept in the trees. When the sun had gone down, and there was no more light by which to paint the day's stories on a wall, Man searched for a place to rest. But they say that, when the light went out, Man got very scared. She no longer trusted what was, in the daylight, her home. She didn't trust what she couldn't see. This anxiety would increase over the millennia, would get so strong that some people would stop trusting altogether what happened in the dark. The phrase "seeing is believing" would get invented, though nearly everyone would misunderstand it. Sleeping on the ground was less work for man, but sleeping on the ground was frightening. Sometimes Man slept on her back and stared at the endless firmament. How much safety there seemed in smallness. As it was told to me, at some point in evolution, Man tried sleeping in trees. High up in the branches, Man could survey her domain. She was that much closer to space, to stars. She saw stars differently from her vantage in the trees, noticed the shapes they made. When she was high enough she found a limb and stretched herself across it. The evening wind blew and Early Man dropped into sleep.

Man slept well for most of the night, they say, and then, at some point, Man lost her balance. Gravity was in charge once again and now Early Man was falling. She clutched at the tree but the tree wasn't there. Helpless, featherless—and what happened when she hit the ground we can't ever know.

I was told that Man once slept in the trees and this is why we have dreams of falling. It's a good theory in any case, an interesting explanation for a phenomenon that makes no sense. How can the experience of a catastrophic fall be intrinsic, when most of us have never fallen this way before?

Carl Jung, the renowned dream translator, had his own theories about falling dreams. He thought that falling dreamers were people with "unrealistic ideas," people of the sort who made "grandiose plans." Jung found that dreamers of falling dreams were also prone to dreams of flying. The falling dream, for Jung, was a warning, a warning to those who try to push beyond their limits. A failure to heed the message of the falling dream could lead to real-life accidents—a tumble down a flight of stairs or a motor crash. In *Man and His Symbols*, Jung recalled the case of a patient who was involved, as Jung put it, in "a number of shady affairs." The patient with the tendency for shady affairs had, in addition, a mania for what Jung called "dangerous mountain climbing," which Jung saw as the man's desire to rise above his self. One night, in a dream, wrote Jung, the man saw himself stepping off the summit of a high mountain and into empty space. Jung told the patient that he was in great peril, that if he did not heed the dream's premonition and start exercising some self-control, the man would surely die.

Six months later, wrote Jung, while on a mountain-climbing expedition, the man with a passion for climbing and shady affairs inexplicably let go of his rope. He landed on his friend, wrote Jung, and dragged them both to their deaths. Later, the man's hiking guide reported the sight. It was as if the man, said the guide, were "jumping into the air."

Toward the end of his life, Pieter Bruegel's paintings were filled with scenes of falling. He seemed obsessed with the various ways a body could fall. Living in the wake of the Reformation, and the initiation of modern times, in the paintings of Pieter Bruegel the whole world is falling. In *The Fall of the Rebel Angels*, open-mouthed fish flop backward upon fish, eggs fall from the wombs of geese and geese fall from the sky, devils fall upon skeletons, frog creatures collapse on their backs and rip open their bellies toward the sun, all the rebel angels tumble. Falling, in this painting, is surrender—the rebel angels defeated. In *The Land of Cockaigne*, a clerk, a peasant farmer, and a soldier have fallen to the ground, overcome, as men can be, by a luscious meal. The soldier lies on his back, head turned like a sleeping baby's. The farmer has fallen over on his side, arms warped the way they never are in waking life. The clerk lies, legs splayed and eyes staring, like a corpse. The fallen figures appear to have lost the will or the ability to move. The Dutch title of the painting, *Het Luilekkerland*, means "The Lazy-Luscious-Land." The Lazy-Luscious-Land is a mythical land of plenty beloved in Dutch literature. It is a place where roast-ed duck flies into your mouth and cheese rains down from the sky. The only way to reach this land is to eat your way through a mountain of pudding. Heavy in body but light in spirit, the clerk, the peasant farmer, and the soldier have collapsed under the weight of abundance. In the Lazy-Luscious-Land, the men are full but are empty.

In *Landscape with the Fall of Icarus*, Bruegel catches Icarus in the most compromised kind of falling, the in-between kind, half fallen and half landed in the sea. His head is submerged and his white legs kick the air after his failed attempt to reach the sun. It's a fair but cool day in the village; the plowman looks to the ground, the shepherd looks up at the sky. But no one sees the fallen boy, struggling to stay afloat. In a few minutes, the broken water will be softly lapping waves.

Perhaps Bruegel's most powerful and weirdest falling painting is *Massacre of the Innocents*. The painting is based on a story in the Gospel of Matthew, in which King Herod orders the slaughter of every male Jewish baby in the vicinity of Bethlehem. Bruegel painted this biblical scene as if it happened in a typical Flemish village. The soldiers in the painting wear the dress of the Spanish army; some are on horseback, in a band in the background, and wait. The season is winter. The villagers are in assorted states of physical despair: a man has dropped to his knees and pleads, a child with one arm drooping gazes up at a soldier, one woman has simply sat down in the snow. There are, however, no innocents to be seen.

It's well known that the painting, like much of Bruegel's work, is a hardly disguised depiction of the atrocities regularly committed in Flanders by mercenaries of Philip II of Spain, the ruler of the Low Countries at that time. A decade after its creation, *Massacre of the Innocents* was acquired by Rudolf II, who liked the painting but disliked the corpses, and so ordered that the slain babies be painted over with ice and snow. Some babies were turned into food or unidentified bundles. One soldier stabs at a turkey, another at a water pitcher. One dead child was turned into a selection of cheeses and hams. Yet Rudolf II's attempts at erasure had the eerie effect of turning back time. No longer was Bruegel's painting about witnessing a massacre that had happened, as the painter intended. Nor was it about a chance meeting between villagers and soldiers, as Rudolf would have it. In the rehashed painting, the villagers' slumping bodies become pleas of deliverance for an event about to happen. With the absence of the children, the survivors become the painting's focus. Bruegel's painting of fallen babies became a painting of bodies in the act of falling. In trying to cancel the events of a holocaust, Rudolf II designed a painting of a holocaust perpetually about to occur.

There's this line by W. H. Auden from the poem "Musée des Beaux Arts": *They never forgot,* the line starts—and Auden is talking about the old masters like Bruegel here—*They never forgot | That even the dreadful martyrdom must run its course | Anyhow in a corner* ... And later in the poem, he writes,

In Breughel's Icarus, for instance: how everything turns away
Quite leisurely from the disaster; the ploughman may
Have heard the splash, the forsaken cry,
But for him it was not an important failure....

In his falling paintings, Bruegel suggests a parallel between falling and ignoring, or, you could say, between falling and forgetting. The ones who are actively falling forget where they have been and can only be absorbed in fallen-ness. The witnesses to the falling, by the same turn, are not involved in falling and so can't be bothered by it. Their falling is an act of willful evasion. The falling is not happening to them; it might as well not exist.

To fall is to forget. To forget is to fall.

When I study the paintings of Pieter Bruegel, I wonder about his mornings and if he had falling dreams like me. Morning is a kind of amnesia too; we drop into asleep, into the abyss, and everything falls away. *We* also fall away, away from ourselves and into ourselves—sleep is paradoxical like that. Sleep is a promise of forgetting, isn't it? A promise that we will open our eyes in the morning and have a new day, leave the previous day and live this one. When the morning comes, it's easy to wake in a state of avoidance, just like Bruegel's plowman, to turn away from yesterday's uncomfortable disaster. Yesterday is still with us, dreams are still with us, all of it on the periphery of our consciousness. We wake in the morning with the sense that there's something we're supposed to do, but this something has no name.

The inevitability of morning grew fainter with each afternoon I awoke with the day half done. For a few hours until dark, I could begin to believe that the world—the world of tomorrows—had evaporated. There is an equanimity in the afternoon when it happens to you from bed. The living world goes on standing, and there you are, existing but indiscernible. You might think it is difficult to drop away from life, but it happens in no time at all. Everything turns away quite leisurely.

✳

This morning, when I looked outside, the branches were finally bare. Seasons change the morning. In November, leaves sail up and drift laterally from one dead branch to another. They are like soldiers in an unfamiliar village who search for a place to rest.

✦

Between 1925 and 1926, Carl Jung lived among a tribe in Mount Elgon, Kenya. The analyst was fifty then. During his time in Africa, Jung made a number of attempts to ask the people of Mount Elgon about their dreams. But the people of Mount Elgon insisted that they did not dream at all. Jung could not believe them and continued his efforts throughout his stay. Jung suspected that the people of Mount Elgon just didn't want to share their dreams with him. Yet, as the days passed and he spent more time speaking with them, the members of the tribe began to open up. They told Jung that they did in fact dream, but that their dreams were meaningless. They told Jung they were just ordinary men, and that the dreams of ordinary men are worthless. The dreams of tribal chiefs and medicine men had meaning, they said, because these people were concerned with the welfare of the entire tribe. Tribal chiefs and medicine men dreamed the collective dream.

On one occasion, Jung met with the healing man, the *laibon*, of the tribe and they talked for a very long time. *Yes*, he told Jung, *in the old days I had dreams*. But now the British were in Kenya, said the man, and no one had dreams anymore. It was the British district commissioner, in charge of the tribe's behavior, who had taken over the responsibility of dreaming. The healing man, dressed in magnificent robes, looked at Jung with tears in his eyes. In the old days, said the *laibon* to Jung, the medicine men knew whether there would be war or sickness, whether rain would come, and where the herds should be driven. But now, he said, dreams were no longer needed because the Englishmen knew everything.

Carl Jung was a scientist of dreams, but he was a collector of them too. Jung had known thousands of dreams. Some dreams in Jung's collection were quickly resolved and soon forgotten. Other dreams lived with Jung for years, haunting him, and Jung would revisit them in the way a grown child returns to a family house, the house shifting and changing with each visit, becoming at once less powerful and more significant. A single dream dreamed by a patient could become a recurring dream for Jung. Not long before he died, in what would be his last essay, Jung came back to a dream—in fact a series of dreams—dreamed by an eight-year-old girl. The story goes like this. One winter, a fellow psychiatrist came to see Jung. The psychiatrist brought with him a book that had been given to him as a Christmas present. It was a book, made by his ten-year-old daughter, of a series of dreams she had when she was eight years old. The psychiatrist told Jung that he found his daughter's book "wholly incomprehensible." Indeed, the Christmas present from daughter to father comprised "the weirdest series of dreams" Jung had ever come across. The images the girl had recorded were childlike, wrote Jung, yet uncanny. Later, in his notes, Jung summarized the dreams:

1. "The evil animal," a snakelike monster with many horns, kills and devours all other animals. But God comes from the four corners, being in fact four separate gods, and gives rebirth to all the dead animals.

2. An ascent into heaven, where pagan dances are being celebrated; and a descent into hell, where angels are doing good deeds.

3. A horde of small animals frightens the dreamer. The animals increase to a tremendous size, and one of them devours the little girl.

4. A small mouse is penetrated by worms, snakes, fishes, and human beings. Thus the mouse becomes human. This portrays the four stages of the origin of mankind.

5. A drop of water is seen, as it appears when looked at through a microscope. The girl sees that the drop is full of tree branches. This portrays the origin of the world.

6. A bad boy has a clod of earth and throws bits of it at everyone who passes. In this way all the passers-by become bad.

7. A drunken woman falls into the water and comes out renewed and sober.

8. The scene is in America, where many people are rolling on an ant heap, attacked by the ants. The dreamer, in a panic, falls into the river.

9. There is a desert on the moon where the dreamer sinks so deeply into the ground that she reaches hell.

10. In this dream the girl has a vision of a luminous ball. She touches it. Vapors emanate from it. A man comes and kills her.

11. The girl dreams she is dangerously ill. Suddenly birds come out of her skin and cover her completely.

12. Swarms of gnats obscure the sun, the moon, and all the stars, except one. That one star falls upon the dreamer.

The father was unable to imagine how his daughter could have come up with these spectacles on her own: images of destruction and regeneration, of darkness and illumination, of sacrifice, of serpents, of baptism; the element of "fourness." Ancient, archetypal images. And so many dreams of falling. The family was not religious, the psychiatrist reminded Jung; the girl was only ten. She had wanted to tell her father something with this book, but he could not understand what. The dreams of his daughter, and her desire to give them as a gift, were mysterious.

There was one other aspect of the dream book Jung found notable. Each dream began with the fairy-tale words "Once upon a time ..." *Once upon a time I saw in my dream an animal that had lots of horns. It spiked up other little animals with them. It wriggled like a snake and that was how it lived. Then a blue fog came out of all four corners, and it stopped eating. Then God came, but there were really four Gods in the four corners. Then the animal died, and all the eaten-up animals came out alive again.* Once upon a time ... and so on. The girl being ten years old, the dreams of her eight-year-old self were already part of her distant past. But they were also part of a past that seemed to precede her. The apparently biblical imagery in the dreams of the girl did not interest Jung; he knew the images were much older than that. The Christlike motif of resurrection and blessing—by water, by stars—appears in many traditions. No one really knows how this story began. *We do not even know,* wrote Jung, *how to go about investigating the problem.* Jung thought perhaps he might talk to the girl himself, but time passed and Jung never got the chance. One year after the Christmas she made a dream book for her father, the girl contracted an infectious disease and died.

There are dreams we have that seem like they belong to someone else. They are like memories of events long forgotten of experiences we never had. Children, whose history is so short, and who have so few memories, can find it easier to see their lives as belonging to a long and mythical tale. We adults think our thoughts are quite original, that our thoughts began when we did, when probably they are closer to myth. Jung wrote that each dream is a direct and intimate message to the dreamer. A dream is the voice of desires and cares that we don't always know or understand. Dreams are sentences seeking a story. They contain themes—"elements," Jung called them—that are almost primordial. Dreams are made from stuff bigger than we are; we inherit dreams in our blood and bones. Dreams contain prehistory and folklore and archetype. To fall in a dream is an individual experience, but Falling comes again and again in dreams, to people and through people, across space and time. This is not just a matter of being part of history. History is culture; it is facts accumulated, language learned, skills acquired. Jung's elements are to be accessed, not learned. The process is closer to trusting our instincts. As birds have an instinct to build nests, so must we dream of falling.

Dreams talk to us, but they are confusing because we don't understand the cryptic language of the dream world. This language is a mess of symbols we once knew a long time ago. *The dream is its own interpretation*, wrote Jung, invoking the Talmud. It is filled with symbolism but is not a symbol. A dream is only what it presents itself to be. Dreams don't lie and they don't disguise. In former times, wrote Jung in *Man and His Symbols, men did not reflect upon their symbols; they lived them and were unconsciously animated by their meaning.* In former times, meant Jung, men did not work their dreams. Dreams worked the men.

I wonder if it has always been this way. As I dream about Early Man's falling, maybe she was dreaming too, dreaming the dreams of an even more ancient creature's bungled attempts at living. One day someone I'll never meet may see just what I saw. They will fall my falling. They say that our lives continue those of the dead before us—maybe we are also dreaming their dreams. Maybe that's why some of our dreams are so incomprehensible. They are not entirely ours.

This is to say that, after the death of his colleague's daughter, Jung couldn't help but wonder if the girl knew she was about to die all along, and that she was trying to tell her father.

Although he often felt defensive of the fact, Jung's approach to dreams was undeniably more mystical than the approach of his colleagues, especially of Freud, his mentor, with whom Jung had become scared to share his dreams for fear of battles over meaning, and indeed Jung did eventually lose Freud's friendship, as the older analyst had come to believe that the younger looked forward to Freud's early death, a thought Freud arrived at after noticing Jung's interest in the mummified corpses of Bleikeller, which the two men visited together in 1909 on their way to catch a boat to America.

Jung's break with Freud shortly before World War I left Jung disoriented and lost—"totally suspended in mid-air" was the phrase Jung used in his memoir. Freud was Jung's intellectual nemesis and he was also Jung's foundation. Jung knew he had to realize his own analytic method but had no idea what that would be. He felt, though, that simply reading other people's minds from an armchair would not help them, and that the only way to understand the message of the elements was to submerge oneself into the bewildering, irrational, and frightening story of dreams.

Sometime in his late thirties, Jung began to have what could only be called apocalyptic visions. It should be mentioned that, in his late thirties, Carl Jung was doing quite well. He had a devoted wife, a family, success in his profession. And still, it was around this especially comfortable period of his life that Jung saw a monstrous flood covering the lands between the North Sea and the Alps. He saw drowned bodies and the rubble of civilization. He saw seas turned to blood. He dreamed of Lorraine and its canals frozen and deserted of human beings, all of it killed by frost. He dreamed of corpses being put into crematory ovens that were then discovered to be alive. On one occasion, Jung dreamed of a girl, who was about eight years old. The girl came and put her arms around Jung and then vanished. In her place was a white dove. The dove, speaking slowly and with the voice of a human, said to Jung, *Only in the first hours of the night can I transform myself into a human being.* Jung kept these visions to himself. He started to worry he might be slipping into psychosis. He lived in fear of losing his mind. Then, on August 1, 1914, war arrived in Europe and Jung's task became clear to him: he must look deep within himself to understand how his experiences related to those of everyone else, to lay bare the strangeness of his own mind.

I have an image of Jung in the office on the second floor of his home, behind a locked door, away from his wife and children, the key in his pocket, obsessively drawing mandalas. I see him writing in his notebooks, plummeting beneath the waves of his own psyche, his cravings, chipping at the wall between reason and soul. I see Jung sitting at his desk lost in a labyrinth without a center. *Sometimes it was as if I were hearing it with my ears*, wrote Jung many years later in his memoir, *sometimes feeling it with my mouth, as if my tongue were formulating words; now and then I heard myself whispering aloud. Below the threshold of consciousness everything was seething with life.* I picture a middle-aged man getting up in the morning, eating breakfast with his family, conducting a thriving psychiatric practice, and wondering if that would be the day he would retreat to his office and never come out again. Once a voice told Jung, *If you do not understand the dream, you must shoot yourself!* Jung thought a good deal about Friedrich Nietzsche during this time, who had traveled a similar journey of the mind. Nietzsche went so far as to devise an entire philosophy of morning, a philosophy that was to liberate people from the stories of dreams and all the stories of people. This total liberation of the individual spirit, it must be said, led the philosopher to inexorable darkness, the darkness of all thinkers who abandon themselves utterly to their own ideas. *I have a medical diploma from a Swiss university, I must help my patients, I have a wife and five children, I live at 228 Seestrasse in Küsnacht*, Jung repeated to himself. These facts of Jung's life, these impingements on his freedom, assured Jung that he truly existed.

Jung often felt that what he was doing in his office at 228 Seestrasse was—as many of Jung's peers believed too—incompatible with his claims to be a scientist and, moreover, crazy. In public, Jung was defensive, but privately he asked himself, *Is this science? Is it nature? Is it art?* I suspect that what Jung actually believed but could not say was that the symbolic life was reality and the systems explaining symbols, illusion. In 1957, just a few years before he died, Jung spoke to a colleague, the Swiss analyst Aniela Jaffé, about his notebooks. *The years of which I have spoken to you*, he told her, *when I pursued the inner images, were the most important time of my life. Everything else is to be derived from this. It began at that time, and the later details hardly matter anymore. My entire life consisted in elaborating what had burst forth from the unconscious and flooded me like an enigmatic stream and threatened to break me…. Everything later was merely the outer classification, scientific elaboration, and the*

integration into life. But the numinous beginning, which contained
everything, was then.

You may have had the occasional suspicion, as have I, that true insanity is our inability to escape order and reason. This finding is confirmed at any asylum. When you speak to the institution-alized, you can find it very hard to argue. Their logic can be rock solid. There is no winning with those who are deemed mentally ill, because they are the least able or willing to let go of their system. This is why the line between fundamentalism and insanity is tenuous. Perhaps the sorrow of Jung is that he felt compelled to make a reflecting pool from the flood of his soul, and despite his attempts to create a scientific method from this torrent of impression and intuition, knew in his heart that with the system came the loss of the ecstasy.

Jung had a vivid memory of a professor who once came to see him in a panic. The professor told Jung of a vision that came "as if from nowhere." After the professor described his mysterious vision, Jung walked over to his shelf. He pulled down a four-hundred-year-old book and opened to a page. On that page was a woodcut with the exact image described by the professor. *There's no reason for you to believe that you're insane*, Jung said to him. *They knew about your vision 400 years ago*. At which point, relates Jung, the professor sat down deflated but returned to normal, at least for the day.

Looking back now, I wonder if I wasn't less interested in de-ciphering my dreams and more interested in what dream books could tell me about what to do when I woke up. I suppose this was Jung's point all along, that the dream world is not separate from the everyday world, that we enact our dreams in daily life as we enact our daily life in dreams, and that to divide these parts of ourselves—the sleeping self and the wide-awake self—makes us incomplete. Who are you in the morning, really? The dreamer or the dreamed? That sunlight is the light of the ancients too; it is yours and theirs together. They are right there, next to the bed, beside you. This floor, this air—in the morning the bedroom is unsettling because it is so crowded.

I can see Jung waking up with his head full of untranslated voyages, waiting for the moment he could open his book again, the illuminated manuscript of his interior life Jung named *The New Book*, (and which would later come to be called *The Red Book*), writing and writing and then secreting the book away in a cupboard until it could be opened the next day. But for all his efforts, the language of dreams remained unattainable to Jung. The morning was always simply morning: reasonable, dependable. The sun was just the sun. Jung's morning ritual was slippers and a newspaper. He had become his own British district commissioner.

The sun—what fills me with such inner exaltation? wrote Carl Jung to himself. *I should not forget my morning prayer—but where has my morning prayer gone?*

Dear sun, wrote Jung, *I have no prayer, since I do not know how one must address you.*

What shall I do this whole long morning?

When I look at the photograph of Jung among the tribesmen of Mount Elgon, with his fragile Swiss knees peeping below his safari shorts, I see an intense melancholy. The tribe's collective morning, which was once a process of remembering, had become a time of forgetting. I don't think anything could have been sadder to Jung than people who had lost their dreams.

4:00 AM

*H*ow many times have I dreamed of this?

✳

I was in the fat chair as usual, in the house on University Circle, watching the screen, when I turned to look across the room. I'm sure it was 4:00 a.m. On the carpet below the wall where the family pictures used to hang, but had since become a display of pale rectangles after my mother left and my father took down the photos, I saw a tiny shadow cast by the light of the television. It was the shadow of a black cockroach. I remember this shadow so well, and remember thinking that cockroaches, who always seem to be running and in a mass—as this is part of what makes them particularly unnerving—also take their time, and desire stillness and solitude. Of course, what drives cockroaches frantic is us, people breaching the contract of the dark morning hours, when it ought to be the cockroaches' time. What I remember most clearly is how this tranquil roach did not seem to notice me at all; for the cockroach, I was furniture, the fat chair and I one being, casting our fatter shadow on the floor. I had the impression that the cockroach manifested spontaneously, but who knows how long it had been there? For how many early mornings had the cockroach vanished and reappeared like that—me, oblivious; cockroach, indifferent? And more important, how many mornings before me? A shadow is a vacancy and it is a premonition; it both follows and precedes. Jung wrote of the *adumbratio*, an anticipatory shadow, that moves over the life and dreams of one who is unknowingly about to die. This *adumbratio* had cast itself over the daughter of Jung's professor friend and she expressed it in a book. What better way to prepare for death than to write a book of shadows? I had the sudden awareness that the cockroach had always been there, at just that hour, for a million years or more. To this day, I'm not sure why this morning was so memorable, the morning I noticed the roach—I can't tell you what was playing on the TV, for instance, or what I had been thinking before the encounter, if my father was in bed or in the hospital. But I can say that the meeting gave me two feelings at once, each one, on the face of it, contradicting the other, but each equally true: the first, that I should not have been there, awake just before dawn in the living room with my encyclopedias on the floor and the desert outside darker than seemed possible; and the second, a feeling I can only describe, though it sounds overblown, as a feeling of loss or, put another way, of discovery, discovery of an otherwise concealed primeval world, one falling back hundreds of millions of years, many millions of years before people, where the boundaries between morning and night were more fluid—the prehistoric cockroach world. I think this must be what Franz Kafka was trying to voice in *The Metamorphosis*, when Gregor Samsa wakes one morning from a troubled sleep to find that he has become a roach. Kafka, a sickly Jew in modern Prague, a contemplative cloistered in an insurance office, chose as his second self a cockroach, a creature so despised, so ordinary, and so visible that it is in fact hidden and, because of that hiddenness, sacred, more connected to that word-less, personless time beyond purity and pestilence. A cockroach is everything because it is nothing.

People often talk about the experience of time standing still. I say this happens at 4:00 a.m. Even the insects stop, even the animals sleep. Four a.m. is the darkest hour, the darkness of predawn, when life seems about to happen but has not yet, when both nature and civilization rest. The sky holds itself someplace between moon and sun, but there is no light to be seen. In the Vedic tradition, I've read, 4:00 a.m. is the luckiest time to rise because it's a time of space. 4:00 a.m. is called the "Creator's Hour" and also the hour of ambrosia. There is an abundance of emptiness at 4:00 a.m.—you can hear yourself and know your intentions more clearly. To rise before dawn is to be awake among the slumbering. There is clarity in the atmosphere. To wake and bathe at 4:00 a.m. is the path to liberation. At 4:00 a.m. in India, I imagine, the birds are sleeping and the sky is black and there is only the periodic echo of a few souls washing.

Artists who have tried to render 4:00 a.m. tend to produce works that are more space than form, more smoke than substance. How does one portray nothing? Let us be clear. When the Wolf comes to us at 3:00 a.m., its task is annihilation. The demons' speech is not intended to disturb us—it is to bring us closer to oblivion. Look at Edward Steichen's photograph of Auguste Rodin's *Balzac* and you will see what I mean. Steichen called the photograph *Balzac, The Silhouette—4 A.M.* This word, "silhouette," implies the outline or contour of a shape, a shape turned to void by light yet a shape nonetheless. In his title, Steichen was assuring us that his Balzac, the Balzac in the photo, was just a representation of the original by Rodin, a reinterpretation, if you will—Balzac cast in a new light. But the more I stare at this photograph, the more I see how Steichen used 4:00 a.m. to gobble Balzac whole, to turn Rodin's massive white plaster sculpture—a sculpture described alternately by critics, when it was first displayed in 1898 at the Paris Salon, as "a block of salt caught in a shower" and "a snowman in a bathrobe whose empty sleeve suggests a strait-jacket," and by the artist himself as "the result of a lifetime"—into a Balzac-shaped hole cut into the horizon. Propped over a precipice, Steichen's is a Balzac one could tumble into and vanish, a Balzac of disappearance. As the story goes, after the disastrous exhibition of 1898, a deflated Rodin relinquished his commission to the Société des Gens de Lettres and took his Balzac back to his studio, where it would reside mostly undercover until more than twenty years after the sculptor's death, when, in 1939, a bronze version of the statue was propped up on the boulevard Raspail, in an attempt to make the Balzac more monumental and less snow-man. But thirty-eight years before that, a young Steichen—who had been greatly impressed when he saw Rodin's sculpture in a Milwaukee newspaper article, thinking it was more a mountain come to life than man—came to visit the aging sculptor, asking to photograph the artist and his works. Steichen's first move was to pull Balzac out of hiding and into the open air of the gardens at Rodin's home in Meudon. It was then Rodin got the idea that Balzac should be photographed by moonlight. The photographer had not tried this technique before, which would require very long exposure times. Yet he was intrigued. For two nights, Steichen sat with the Balzac, watching the form with his camera eye. On the first night, he took a picture at exactly 11:00 p.m. On the second night, the photographer stayed longer, from sunset to sunrise, following the moonlight as it passed across the sky, and at 4:00 a.m. took his second photo. So what seems like an instant in *The Silhouette—4 A.M.* is in fact the physical evidence of time passing. Or you could flip this idea around. As the night passed, Rodin's sculpture of Balzac slowly dissolved until finally culminating in this one true moment you could call emergence by negation, and also 4:00 a.m.

As the story goes, Rodin was thrilled with Steichen's rendering of his Balzac. He proclaimed that it was Steichen who would make people understand his sculpture. Rodin told Steichen that his photographs reminded him of "Christ walking in the wilderness." Rodin, who had devoted his life to material and form and mass, wanted only to see what his sculptures looked like as emptiness. And Steichen, who was able to invoke the powers of the moon to turn plaster into shadow, could still not resist, when his photograph was done, signing it in bold yellow crayon.

When I was a child, there were many books on the shelf in the living room, on the wall between the fat chair and the television, that no one ever read. The encyclopedias, for example. The Bible. A baby book my mother had made for my brother when he was born that detailed his milestones and accomplishments. My parents' wedding album. I would flip through the Bible sometimes and read the opening lines of Genesis, but never got much past them. I never could grasp how God's first act of creation could be formlessness. The first act of God, it seemed, was not to make heaven and earth, as is sometimes believed, but an amorphous emptiness named "heaven and earth." Was that which God created first the *idea* of earth and heaven? Because before Something we needed Nothing from which Something could emerge? In the beginning, God created heaven and earth, and then the next line is, *Now the earth was formless and empty, darkness was upon the face of the deep, and the Spirit of God hovered over the waters.* Whenever I read this line I was filled with an immense sadness for this God, the God of Genesis, a formless Spirit over a formless Nothing. In time, I came to understand from these lines that the world unfolded from God's loneliness, a hovering loneliness exhaling over a formless earth and a heaven that had no purpose. Yet what happens next is significant. Before the creation of any living soul to keep God company, before water and before the sky, before all the things that God deems good, God turns on the lights. The light doesn't come from the sky because the sky is made later. The vault of the sky comes from the light and not the other way around. Light, and not heaven—light, and not earth—is God's first true creation. And not really light but rather *emergence*, the emergence of light from dark. Before there is a world, before goodness or life, God creates emergence and time. Meaning this: before goodness or life, before world, God makes the morning. Morning, like Creation, is not static; morning is a becoming. God saw that the light was good, but then separated the light from the darkness, an abiding separation that God called the night. Everything that follows springs from this rupture: the seeds and the animals and the people. According to this interpretation of Creation, it must be said, we are not children of light but of estrangement. And before we read any further, we are told, we must remember this: the stories that follow are about this fracture, the beauty and the sadness of Creation.

✳

I have a sincere admiration for people who can rearrange their furniture. Every time I want to move the furniture around I can't seem to do it. The things, once placed, are home. At least, this is my belief. I never know exactly why, when I put a new object on the windowsill, a photo on the wall, the thing goes where it does. Having little sense of interior design, I don't deliberate much about where a thing will go when it comes into a room. The thing guides me to a location and there it stays. Or I choose randomly and there it stays. Anyway, the intention is less lasting than the placement. A friend of mine changes up her furniture annually, according to her mood, and even though I tend to like the way her furniture used to be, I also find the newly arranged rooms undeniably refreshing.

Every person's home is a private museum. Museums, almost more than anything else, encapsulate humanist philosophy perfectly: that all things are utterly connected, utterly mysterious, and that, when put into the hands of humans, will become arbitrarily, beautifully, and often poorly organized. Nearly everyone believes things have a story to tell; the question is whether you think that people impart stories to things or divine the stories from them.

I've come to realize that my attachment to my things is not only reflected in the stories I've given them, many of which are quite elaborate; I am also attached to my things' location in space. I tend to believe that this or that thing had no meaning before I took it home and placed it just so—lonely, unhappy thing! lying there in a box or forced to stand at attention among deceptively similar things. I use things to decorate my house, but secretly I want the things to become the architecture of my soul. What a heavy load to place on them. Poor things. Things are only illustrations of my identity, I know; they can't be a substitute for me. I can have a relationship to my things but I am not them, and we cannot own each other. Once, long ago, it was different. Prehistoric people knew that things had a life of their own. When did we stop believing in the life-world of things?

Whenever I return from traveling, I feel a dread as I approach home. I worry that the things won't be as they were when I left them and that, as a result, I will be returning to the stranger's house, that the things will no longer be mine. Have you ever had the feeling when you woke up in the morning that the bed had changed position?

This experience is not unlike the day Imre Kertész described in his novel *Fatelessness*, when a teenage boy named Georg, a boy based on Kertész himself, comes back to Budapest after a year in the concentration camps. There Georg stands, in front of the Western Railway Terminal, his city familiar but aloof. *Outside... the sun was blazing down straight onto the sidewalk. The heat, noise, dust, and traffic were prodigious. The streetcars were yellow, with a No. 6 on them, so that had not changed either. There were vendors too, selling odd-looking pastries, newspapers, and other goods. The people were very good-looking, and palpably all of them had some errand, some important business; all were hurrying, rushing, running somewhere, jostling, in all directions.* Earlier that day, Georg has an opportunity to examine his face in a mirror. The face he sees is unlike the face he recalled from days past. The forehead of this face is lower, the ears amorphous, the eyes beady and shrunken.

I never heard these kinds of homecoming tales from my family, as none who stayed in Europe survived the war. But I had a desire once, in the winter of 2008, to find the house in Poland my grandmother left as a child. All I had to go on was a ten-year-old's memory wrapped in a ninety-year-old mind and an address that my grandmother kept safe in a mental pocket until the day she died. Yet even with this insubstantial bit of information, I was confident I would find the house in Lublin and, moreover, confident it would be just as I had imagined, my imagination's translation of my grandmother's memory. Needless to say, when I got there, to this address in Poland that was my grandmother's childhood home, I found a postwar brick building filled with Polish people eating McDonald's hamburgers that was, in fact, a McDonald's. This incident can't simply be blamed on war or even history. We are departing at every moment, returning at every moment, and if there is any lesson to be learned in this life it's that nothing stays the same because nothing is ever as it was. We know this every time we try to recollect a street, try to preserve our faces, try to live now in a world that is gone and experience the past in the present.

Reason tries to comfort me whenever I leave home and come back, telling me that all will be well, all will be stable, that my things have no life of their own, that their identities rely on me, that I can rely on the stability of things. But then there's a new cobweb in the corner, new dust gathered on the books. The molecules have shifted, and I myself am not the same when I enter again through the front door. I am also an ever-changing thing. Often, when I return from traveling, I'm sure that the objects in my home have moved from where they were, and as I start the process of putting them back in their original spots, I invariably see that the things have not moved, could not have moved without doing so of their own accord, and that my memory of where the things had been was false.

In the days of morningless mornings the placement of things was important. Things were my lighthouses and so could not be moved without inviting shipwrecks. When I opened my eyes into the new day, the first thing I saw was things. I saw the heavy light blue curtains drawn over the windows, to keep out the neighbors and the sun; I saw the music posters on the ceiling and the stacks of records I had rescued from the streets; I saw the white plastic alarm clock that had gone yellow; I saw the rocks collected from the desert piled on the desktop; I saw the mirror over the dresser that reflected the room; I saw the closet and the floor; I saw the stuffed animals on the dresser I hadn't spoken to for some time and the television that had been put in my bedroom a couple of years before. Yet almost every day, for the first second or two of waking, when the alarm clock rang at noon and the desert sun was already high, the things were foreign to me. I wasn't quite sure what it all was—the objects, the bed, the house, or who I was among them.

✳

Even now, no matter what time I wake or where, there is a part of me that wakes by the closed window at noon.

✳

Have you noticed how you can wake in the morning surrounded by people and they can't ever know where you've been? Last night, I disappeared for hours—did you see me go? But in the morning, I returned. *Here I am,* I say, *I've come back, listen,* but the trip falls to pieces in words. How many people can surround us when we meet the day, and still when we wake we wake alone. There we are, millions of us in every city there is, lying in our bedclothes at the end of the journey, our private flight back from space, unable to tell each other.

Loren Eiseley once wrote about the seeker of prophetic visions. He wrote that, in all religious thought, no matter how archaic, the seeker of visions must go apart from family and friends, and live for a while in the wilderness. Perhaps the seeker must travel to some unique and sacred place. The world is fantastic, wrote Eiseley, and has been fantastic for so long. We just take the queerness for granted. We rush around *like Mad Hatters upon our peculiar errands, all the time imagining our surroundings to be dull and our-selves quite ordinary creatures. Actually, there is nothing in the world to encourage this idea,* wrote Eiseley, *but such is the mind of man.* So we find it necessary, from time to time, to send emissaries into the wild, hoping they will reappear and tell us of the great events in store for us that will resuscitate our "waning taste for life." The newspaper, the internet, the radio, the television—none of these will give us the information we crave. Only a person, gone away, can tell us. The right sort of searcher will come back from a pilgrimage and present us with a message. *It may not be a message from the god he set out to seek, but even if he has failed in that particular, he will have had a vision or seen a marvel, and these are always worth listening to and thinking about.*

The classic pilgrim travels in search of enlightenment or holiness, like the journey to Mecca, or Santiago de Compostela, or Varanasi. In the writings of Thomas Merton is a different account, however, a singular form of pilgrimage carried out by sixth-century Celtic monks. These pilgrims no longer followed a specific path to Jerusalem or some designated holy site. Instead, they walked a path to no-place. In this era, the era of *peregrinatio*, pilgrimage was self-imposed exile. The Celtic monks became outcasts by choice. They set off to unknown places, often to a forlorn island, without any goal other than to go. Sometimes the monks would land on an island of seabirds; other times the destination was not isolated but filled with natives speaking queer words, and this consummated the pilgrims' alienation. It was not a monument, or a sacred body of water, or a destiny to fulfill, but the lack of any goal that made the *peregrinatio* significant. The "going forth into strange lands" was not a summons to seekers hoping to secure the message. It was a total abandonment to fate. The Celtic monks, following Abraham, wanted to dwell in their desert. Like Abraham, they willingly suffered what is among the worst punishments there is, homelessness, though in the case of *peregrinatio*, theirs was not just an exile from home but from purpose. I wonder if you could call this kind of pilgrimage a voyage without hope. How can you hope if you have no thing to hope for?

I think about these Celtic pilgrims sailing randomly around the choppy North Sea, vulnerable and sick, and then arriving at some island having no idea what to do next. What interests me most is how, for the *peregrinus*, the journey never ends. At first, it seemed to me that going back home to Ireland might be the most difficult part of a *peregrinus*'s experiment, until I learned that they didn't. Once on their island, the pilgrims stayed pilgrims forever. They never had to go back, never had to explain themselves, never had to walk into a village and be unrecognized or to be recognized for one's past self. They never had to examine their face in the mirror, confront the pain of being reabsorbed into normal daily life. For the Celtic monks of sixth-century Ireland, exile and home were the same. In other words, the Celtic monks of sixth-century Ireland lived in perpetual apocalypse.

It might be true, as Eiseley said, that no miracle can withstand a radio broadcast. Perhaps this is why the *peregrini* stayed elsewhere; maybe they were afraid that any miracles they found in exile would dissolve on familiar shores. Even still, according to Eiseley anyway, one must return to the company of people for the message to be fulfilled. This, for me, is the crux of the waking moment; it is a forced homecoming. In sleep, we give ourselves to the unknown. Every night we set off in a rudderless boat and every morning we come back from the inexplicable sea of dreaming. We close our eyes and walk into the desert. I am afraid sometimes that, in sleep, I don't exist, that if I let myself go, I won't exist, that I will become a hologram, that I was never much more than that. When the morning comes I am, for a moment, homeless. How can you know your true home once a pilgrimage ends? Life can never be the same. At the waking moment I must re-exist, must reanimate this body with myself, reanimate this self with my body, just as a phoenix lives for centuries and one day bursts into flames and rises from the ashes and is alive again. The inevitable repetition of morning forces us to come home again and again. If we go away and do not come back, it's like we stayed asleep. Falling asleep is like the start of a pilgrimage, but waking is the lonely return.

There's a word for vampires and ghosts and most of the creatures that haunt us. The word is "revenant," derived from the Latin *reveniens*, though some believe it has its roots in the Norse *aptrgangr*, which is one who walks again. Revenants are those who have died and roam; they are the living dead. The revenant is the instantiation of our greatest desire and also our greatest horror: that the expired will return to us one day but not as they once were. Still, a revenant is not a monster per se; it can also be a person who has come home. *Reveniens* simply means "returning." And if we have gone away from ourselves, even for just a night, when we return, we are revenants too.

Again and again, morning comes—there's just no end to morning. The road from sleep to morning, like a pilgrimage, is a circle that looks like a line.

*

Sometimes I imagine a community of morning where the stories of sleep could be shared. Isn't the message of morning the one all seekers find? That human beings are not so ordinary, that simply waking is incredible.

Whoever dreamed the first dream must have been the loneliest of all.

*

I dream often of the house on University Circle. In my dreams, the house is defined by its parts. It is not a complete structure, you see, but disconnected rooms existing outside of time. Usually I dream of the closet in my childhood bedroom. In my dreams the closet is very long and filled with clothes. In my dreams I stare endlessly at these clothes, which sometimes include costumes. I can't ever pick which outfit to wear. I'm not even sure the clothes are mine. There are times when I dream of another closet, the storage closet next to the laundry room. I've never dreamed about the living room, where I spent so many hours as a teenager. I suppose this room was erased because I was there so often. It became more me than room.

I want to say there was a moment when I knew the days in my father's house were over. Or when it was, exactly, that my father's insomnia ended and my long nights began. When I think of it now, so many years past, I wonder if I had taken on the burden of my father's sleeplessness. The terrors that kept us all awake seemed to dissipate during the time my father and I were alone, and night by night he slept. Did I believe the demons could pass from him and then through me and away? I suppose, though it may be unsatisfying, that the decision to leave was just as unintentional as the resolution to stay. I had only the barest vision of myself in the future. I could see myself sometimes on a train or a boat. What did people in England do? Yet though I could not have said this, I simply knew: as morning must return, so I had to return to it.

In Ovid's version of the tale, Icarus is overjoyed to fly with the wings his father, Daedalus, has fashioned in order to set the boy free. All the wide sky is open to Icarus, steering him straight toward the sun. When he flies too close and drops into the dark sea, Icarus calls out his father's name. Daedalus does not appear in Bruegel's painting. But you can still see him in the shepherd's upward gaze.

The mood in the casino gets more electric the closer it gets to dawn. It's then the casino will surge with the gambler's excitement and desperation; the knowledge that morning is coming and that, when it does, the casino and its logic will vanish. But when the morning does come, and the amateurs dissipate, the true gamblers play on and with even more intent, and play like there is no time.

dawn

*T*he summer I turned nineteen, I woke up most often in the front seat of my car, on the side of a road somewhere. I was moving east that year. There wasn't anyone waiting for me in the East; it was just the place I was going.

I slept in my car partly to save money but mostly to be close to my things, the few things from the house in Las Vegas I had managed to keep with me. When I had told him I was leaving, my father became frightened and began to yell. I gathered what I could, filling suitcases with paper and blankets and clothes, and left. The back seat of my car was piled to the windows with things. This made it impossible to sleep in the back. I had a notion that, when I reached the East, I would go to New York City. I thought I might enroll in school there, though I didn't have a very sound idea of what I would do once enrolled.

In fact, I did reach New York eventually. One afternoon, about two months after I first arrived, I was walking back from class registration—intending to take my car to a service station outside of town, thinking it would be a safer place to sleep than the East Village—when I saw two men on the corner of West Twelfth Street and Seventh Avenue lugging, with difficulty, the suitcases filled with my things. It was only hours later, sitting on a metal bunk bed in a spare and slightly moldering room at the Salvation Army where, exhausted by the events of the day, I had chosen to stay the night, that I realized I had successfully grabbed my suitcases back from the men (who had been very surprised by my actions, to say the least) but had missed the embroidered handbag holding most of what I had written since the age of eight, including a notepad I kept as a teenager that was a written account of my dreams. And, though I'm loath to admit it, for nearly a decade later, long after I had finished college or had any reason to be in that neighborhood, I would go by the corner of West Twelfth Street and Seventh Avenue sometimes, and I would scan the dumpsters—not going so far as to open them, but glancing around their edges, looking down inside if the lids happened to be up—still believing I would find my bag, a bag worthless to the men who had taken it. Why did I care? It was as if I were searching for evidence, but of what I don't know. That corner is totally different now. An entire hospital has been torn down and replaced with luxury condominiums.

If the weather was wet, on the long drive east, I would park the car and pass the night in the driver's seat. Nothing can wake you if you sleep in a car because a car does not let you sleep. It doesn't matter how many hours you spend in it or how tired you are. If the weather was wet, I might spend the night writhing around half dreaming in the driver's seat, but if the weather was fine I would pull over to the side of the highway, leave the towering billboards and their philosophies behind, and I would go into the weeds. There is no place anymore that belongs to no one, and yet it is easy to hide in plain sight just about anywhere in America. The housing developments and mini-malls sprawl over the horizon, but not far from any American roadside is a high patch of weeds you can dive into and disappear. The anonymous American roadside is a hinterland of secrets. If the weather was fine and the weeds were dry, I would spread a blanket on the ground and watch the stars emerge from the shadow of the sun. I could forget about the suitcases full of books and things and the people sleeping in houses. I could forget that everything I owned in the world was both prey to the roadside and worthless, and I could sleep, because no one was waiting for me in the East and so there was nothing to be done in the morning.

For all my short life I had thought of myself as a night person, as a resident of the night. At nineteen, I wore a lot of layers and sleeves. Back home, in the desert, I would wait all day for the sun to go. Then, when the city had tucked itself in, I would join with the other nighttime creatures: the cockroaches, the scorpions, the moon. Sometimes, outside in the yard, I tried to find shapes in the stars: Cassiopeia holding on to her chair and spinning; Ursus the Bear chained to the cosmos. I didn't yet realize that I was not alone with the bugs and the stars, that Las Vegas was filled with night dwellers like me, that people had come from everywhere just to lurk in the shiny corners of Las Vegas. I didn't have anything to do with those people; they were in a different world just a few miles away. But we were the same.

There was one morning on the road, it must have been around 5:00 a.m. This is the hour when light wakes you in summer, the scant light that comes just before sunrise, a diffuse, flimsy light that moves through the air more like a scent than a sight, a light that only birds can hear coming unless you are sleeping outside. Waking light is not like the other light we see. It is not light we witness but light we take in. Our eyes absorb waking light as it rises up out of the weeds. Waking light invades us, floods us, and takes the place of our dreams. It is the light of sensation, that's what I want to say—you can see it just as well with your eyes closed. In the light's early breaths, the eye does not actively see but is a receptacle for sight. Light appears into the early morning and occupies space, takes its place from wherever it spent the night. It rests on the side of that building, in just that one spot, and spreads itself across the surface, until the building and the ungraspable stuff of light are one, and you can't tell anymore what is surface and what is light until sundown arrives and peels the two lovers apart.

But I did not know this then.

One morning when I was nineteen, I woke at 5:00 a.m. and found myself outside, on the ground. You have to understand, at this time in my life, I was drifting between islands. I was a captainless boat. The United States is so vast—you can drive along every detour and never arrive. There will always be the gas station in the spot of town where there are no trees, with its postcards of points of interest miles away, a coffee pot half filled for days, and a gas station attendant whose heart is too fragile. The grass around me was high. I couldn't hear a sound, not even of the cars on the road. I opened my eyes a bit more, and through a short clearing in the weeds, I saw an animal. It was a cat, but more than a cat, like several cats put together. I understand now, many years later, that the cat I saw was a lynx. The way the cat was watching me, I knew it sensed my lack of direction. I looked into its eyes and as I did, I felt that I was seeing something I shouldn't or, worse, something that wasn't there. Even the people of the Mojave, who had once slept where I was sleeping, knew about the lynx but hardly ever saw it, and for this reason, the animal had, over time, become associated with ghosts, although sometimes the lynx would appear to the people of the Mojave in their dreams. The word "lynx" is derived from the Greek word *leukos*, which comes from the Indo-European root *leuk-* and means light, illumination, a reference to the reflective qualities of the cat's eyes, the way light seems to shine from them. What was it Marina Tsvetaeva wrote? *Black*

as—the centre of an eye, the centre, a blackness | that sucks at light.
Plutarch purportedly thought the light in the eyes of a lynx was
so strong it could radiate into solid forms, and for a long time,
because of Plutarch, naturalists believed that the lynx could see
right through rocks and trees. The sky was starting to break
around me. Above, a bird was singing. And all at once, I had the
feeling of walking down a long corridor that was drawing closer
and closer around me with each step. My heart was beating fast;
the ground beneath was unsteady. *I'm in a field, in the Plains some-*
where, I told myself, still staring at the cat. And then I thought the
cat was watching over me because it believed I was a ghost.

Tell me, what is the dawn? Dawn seems like day yet there is no
sun; it seems like night but it isn't dark. The dawn is a threshold,
a split in space-time, a crack in the cosmos; perhaps this is what
is meant by the word daybreak. For one moment, in each span of
twenty-four hours, the universe is broken. Daybreak is not just a
point in time, the period between night and day. It is a rupture in
time, the rupture of Creation reiterating itself. Day can't just
arrive, passing over tranquilly from night. The night must be halted
from proceeding by dawn. If dawn did not break the night, the
night might go on eternally. The dark might perpetuate, might
take over the world, and we would all live and die inside the king-
dom of night. The dawn turns night into a precipice that must
be jumped across. To make the journey from night into morning
we must leap from one to the other. We must hurl ourselves over
the break of day and trust that we will make it. Every day we leap
across an invisible abyss: we, the birds, and everything. *At the hour*
of daybreak it grows colder, wrote Aleksandr Blok. *At the hour of*
daybreak a dark sky. There is a reason vampires fear the threshold.

Dawn is the time of choices. At dawn, all is possibility. All is light and emergence. I suppose what I am trying to say is that dawn is the time of doubt. What is the wish for immortality if not a wish to sleep through the break, to sleep through the doubt of dawn? When we wake at dawn we feel the disquietude of life on the brink, of life temporarily delayed as it dangles over the edge. Have you ever asked yourself how the birds can sing so early? The music of dawn is not like the birdsong of late morning, song of work and sun. The birds of dawn sing in the dark, in anticipation of light. I think the birds are nervous at this hour; they know something imperceptible to us. In winter, with the window closed, it is harder to hear the birds, easier to pretend that they are not there, just outside the window, calling. When the windows are open, or when you sleep outside, it is not so easy to pretend. The window can't protect us then from the advancing of the dawn. Maybe the birds, held between yesterday and today, are calling out to us in the hope that we will give them comfort and company. Rarely do we experience the break of day as the birds do. Sunrise grows nearer, moves closer, the space gets closer and the birds are forced to touch it. Perhaps the wailing of the birds at daybreak is the ballad of the trauma of dawn.

I'm not sure if you've seen this painting, *Rock Arch in the Uttewalder Grund*. I've seen it only in pictures myself. Caspar David Friedrich painted *Rock Arch in the Uttewalder Grund* in the first year of the nineteenth century. It is a landscape in sepia tones, meaning it is colorless. The painting is stuffed with two massive mountains, and between them is a crack of light. A pile of boulders has fallen in the crack but stopped falling just seven feet or so above the ground. The boulders create a vaulted passage of stone and standing in the passageway are two figures. One figure is a small man, and next to him, a man smaller still. Probably it is a boy. The boy is half contorted with wonder. His head is bent back and his arms are raised. He would see the sky but above him is a pile of rocks. The man is turned to us, pointing in the direction of us but past us, toward ... what? He is reaching with that arm, reaching and grasping; even he is not sure what is before him. And what is most remarkable in this painting that is mostly rocks is the way the man and boy hardly appear and yet are so very present. A painting of rocks ought to be a painting of darkness, but the figures are surrounded by light. They are consumed by the light of dawn. The bodies of the man and boy are disappearing inside the light. Dawn passes through them and radiates out of them, has turned them into conduits of morning. To stand before the dawn's big light, this painting says, is to be dominated by its colossal mass. It is to stand helpless and amazed and small before the threat of being utterly crushed.

Later, I rolled up my blanket and found a truck stop restaurant on the other side of the field. I locked up my car and went to the bathroom to wash myself in the sink. I often felt the presence of my car around my body following a long stretch of travel. I wondered if the truck drivers felt like their trucks. I remember the truck stop restaurant was big and white and airy, the kind of truck stop that makes you believe you could drive your truck right into it and continue on to heaven. The sunlight was already strong. How quickly the day moves forward. Morning shined through the big windows onto the truck stop cutlery. There were three or four truck drivers seated inside, and music playing over the clinking of forks. Every driver had a booth of his own, so I picked my own booth too. They are night dwellers also, the truckers, trawling the roads at Wolf Time to make speed across the country. The truckers were tall men, and wide, with bellies that pressed against the tables as they hunched their heads over stacks of waffles and pancakes and sausages and eggs. One walked over to the jukebox and put on a slow song. The waitress set a plate before me. Lined along the edge of my plate were three or four large paper cups of butter. The sight of this butter stays with me today. I remember wondering, What does one do with so much butter? Build something, maybe. A butter castle or a butter wishing hat that turns truck tires into wings and drivers into birds who can sail over the superhighways of the West, to a meadow with flowers, where they can rest their bellies on the grass and spend the night in branches like birds do. The sight of a big man before a plate of waffles is special, because waffles turn back time and make a man little again. I thought I should donate my butter cups to the truckers, as I didn't feel able to handle so much butter on my own, but I could not get any of them to meet my eyes. I called the waitress over and ordered extra toast. When it came, I wrapped the toast in a napkin and put it into my pocket. I had generally thought of myself as either in a place, or not in a place, or ever in search of a place. I never thought that I myself could be a place, a place where morning, for example, could happen.

At the truck stop, I finished my coffee and said a private farewell to my friends. Back in my car, I decided to take a side road, to drive through the town that hosted the truck stop and not much else. Roadside towns all boast something. As I passed their houses, the people of the town were just starting. Televisions were turned on, newspapers taken from front lawns, every house a private performance of morning.

＊

Somewhere, we're told, there's a big, beautiful stillness, a silent forever, maybe even inside us, and we can hear it if not for the clocks inside our heads, ticking away. Even in the casino we are the devoted minions of time. In sleep, we meet infinity but just can't grasp it, because we are too asleep. Morning, then, might be the part of day in which we are most aware of time; morning is the shock of moving from timelessness to time, or, anyway, what we perceive as timelessness and time. In attempting to erase the morning, I wasn't only trying to sidestep time's authority, to lessen the shock of day. I was trying to experience the timelessness I felt only in sleep. I knew back then, without knowing, that there would be some consequence to my rearranging of the hours. I guess this was Jung's scheme too. Inducing dream states in the afternoon was a way of testing the boundaries of morning. Perhaps this is why Jung eventually turned to art and myth.

Every morning at dawn, wrote Jung when he had become an old man, and fonder of chopping wood than writing, the tribespeople of Mount Elgon left their huts and breathed or spat into their hands. They stretched out their hands to the rising sun and offered it their breath and spit. When Jung asked the people of Mount Elgon why they did this, they were baffled by the question. We have always done it, they told Jung. It has always been done.

That first fall, when I reached New York City, I often found myself striking up conversations with homeless men (I never saw any homeless women that year). I would sit beside them and listen to their stories, which sounded the same to me. It is the story of selective history a person reserves for passersby. When the snow fell and holidays came, I baked cookies. I walked around the Upper East Side with my cookies and passed them out to the men. I could have explained this to others as a form of altruism, but to be frank, it felt more like research than charity. These men had taken my experiments with living on the fringes of regulated time to a higher level. In the open air, surrendered to the seasons with nowhere to be, they seemed to know more than just about anyone else what one's own shadow looks like all the way from dawn to dusk.

During the time of morningless mornings, I turned off the alarm on the white plastic clock radio that had gone yellow and never turned it on again. I don't know how long it took my body to find its own pattern of wakefulness and sleep. Not long. My days felt as natural lived in reverse as they did in forward motion. More so, really, perhaps because I had chosen the arrangement of my own free will. Free will makes solitude simple. Pulling up your anchor and setting out to sea is not the same as being cut off from the shore. The boat is the same, the water is the same, but everything is different. A boat adrift is lonely but too detached to be forsaken. In the days of morningless mornings I didn't need an alarm because my brain woke on its own around noon or one o'clock, and at that time, I had nowhere to be.

Have you ever considered the evolution of alarms, how they've gone from birds to clocks? If you could chart the overall develop-ment of alarms on an evolutionary diagram, from the beginning of alarms to now, it would look like the great wide cosmos with its multitude of fiery spirals being gradually shrunken to a sun, then to a bird, and finally to a plastic alarm clock on a bedside table in a teenager's room in Las Vegas. When I was a teenager, I hardly traveled anywhere. But sometimes, on the television at night, movies would show morning in town squares in other parts of the world. Bells would ring from the center of the square through every window in town, or sometimes morning songs. And after, there would be another scene, of people slowly gathering, leaving their homes together, and moving into the streets.

twilight

*B*irds.

How can you sing like that, first off in the morning, when the air is dull and the ground frozen? Do you know by instinct or practice that the early-morning air carries your song farther and louder? By the morning's end the sun bursts in. The chatter of the people erupts and the honking of cars and the screaming of children in the schoolyard. Birdsong breaks apart and vanishes like a handful of confetti blown into an alleyway.

Birds.

There are places where people still sing morning songs like the birds, you know. They call across the sky and make the morning feel large. They are songs of rejoicing that we've made it one more day. I don't know how people can even speak in the morning, not to mention sing. I can hardly believe when I open my eyes that the planet is still revolving, that this room is just how I have left it, that life itself continues. This is it, we say to ourselves each morning—the blank page, the new beginning. Top of the mountain and over the edge. Did you take your morning songs from the ancients, birds, or was it the other way around? The morning is the promised land.

✳

Do you remember when, my love, over a few mornings, you read to me lines from a poem by Marina Tsvetaeva? We were sitting on the bed. I could hear a call to prayer winding through the blare of a morning train going somewhere, and then the horn was lost in snow. You read to me Tsvetaeva's sleepless nights, her solitary wanderings through the enormous streets of Moscow, and her numinous encounters with windows: windows whispering music, windows filled with light, a window that led to a room where two people drank or held hands as three candles burned. In words, at night, Tsvetaeva became a looming, superterrestrial figure, Earth's guest, a visitor come down from above. She spied on the forests and the sleepy cows and the watchman with his hand in the grey fur of a dog. She opened doors to the wind and the rising river tides and cried, *Don't sleep!*

She wrote: *Once asleep—who knows if we'll wake again?*

She wrote: *Don't sleep! Be firm! Listen the alternative is— everlasting sleep. Your—everlasting house!*

Did Tsvetaeva really walk around the streets of Moscow at night? I wanted to know. So much of Russian truth is parable. She may have written this poem in exile, eating horsemeat in a Parisian suburb before her husband was arrested and executed, before her daughter was to die for lack of food, and her other daughter arrested and forced to live, and her son left to see her hanging. Tsvetaeva's voice, in this poem, is less like that of a traveler and more like a misplaced angel. She was a heavenly figure moving through midnight, gathering information about human ways for the single purpose of poetry. Tsvetaeva, too, was a watcher. Her poem is a poem of watching and a love poem to living. Tsvetaeva feared being infinite but secretly longed to be boundless.

She wrote: *Pray for the wakeful house, friend, and the lit window.*

Tonight I hold all the keys to this ... and lack of sleep guides me on my path.

✴

In the desert, twilight is the disappearance of stars. In Las Vegas, the stars disappear and the light bulbs fade, bringing a brief but commanding halt to the city's show: money is put on the nightstand, a glass is set down, a stained cuff is buttoned. A person walking to the car notices, for a brief interlude, how the mountains are blacker than ever against the blue. This blue is a primordial blue, a pre-cloud blue, a blue of the reflection of the cosmos upon the planet, the light over the fishermen's boats. This is not a blue of water and ice—not even a blue of sky. It is the blue of nameless causes, of infinitesimal energies; a blue about which the only thing to say is that it is blue and you can't even say that. It is a blue that lifts like a theater curtain, revealing a thin line of water that drips from a roof gutter and wears away at a patch of brick, a man riding an otherwise empty bus, a woman standing at her car with her keys in her hand unable to go inside, a horse that has gone to stand in the road before someone takes her back. One late-summer day in 1871, in a seaside town he would go to, Bram Stoker thought, *I would like to steal back a moment in the twilight and whisper a prayer in some child's ear,* a wish that the child would be happy and not lonely just by hearing Stoker's prayer. The unspeakable blue of twilight breaks the horizon apart and then whispers, *Darkness is moving away.* And I can tell you that twilight, in Sanskrit, literally means "a holding together," but it really means, as far as I can tell, a junction, a union, a crossroads, a frontier. Twilight is convergence, the place where all roads meet.

✳

There are places like Greenland and Siberia and Alaska where residents often wake to the same darkness in which they fell asleep, or are forced to fall asleep in the unceasing light of day, and I wonder, does this count as morning? Because how could Nature make a morningless place? How much is light morning and how much of morning is light? How can a morning become morning if it advances further into the black? Maybe, on mornings like this, Arctic people make their own internal light out of the memory of sunrises past. In school we learned that the first sun we see at sunrise is a ghost sun, that the light is a ghost light. It is the light we think we see. The actual sun moseys above the horizon a couple of minutes after we are sure we've seen it rise. Every sunrise, every morning, is part reality and part mirage.

And what of the mornings when the sun hasn't set, when light emerges from light? On these mornings, I think, morning must contain, paradoxically, even more darkness than the mornings with no sunrise. On these mornings, I think, mornings of perpetual sun, the sun must carry with it all the afflictions of missing night.

Waking at noon, I could see from my bed the landscape of University Circle through a crack in the heavy blue curtains: the houses neatly placed along the curve of the cul-de-sac, the black asphalt a pond at its center. The cul-de-sac faced a gated housing development you were not allowed to enter. The houses in the development were white and enclosed on every side by a white cinder block wall that was whiter in the midday sun. And beyond the housing development, mountains. I could see the mountaintops the way the slender masts of ships appear on the other side of the window in Friedrich's *Woman at the Window*. In Friedrich's painting, we can see the tops of the ships unmoving on the river Elbe, but the ships themselves are invisible to us and the river is barely there. The woman at the window is in the middle of the painting, leaning over the sill. Her face is unseen, like the ships. On the shore, across the away, Friedrich painted a line of trees. The trees are just starting to bud. I suppose it must be spring. Morning has passed; daylight has arrived. In this painting, I can see the fifteen minutes before the painting, the woman carefully measuring out the end of breakfast, tidying the plates, saying goodbye to her family, her attention pulled toward the window. In this painting, there is the landscape and there is the woman, and between them are an enormous wall, a tall unreachable window, and, beneath it, the open square of a wooden shutter turned back. The way Friedrich painted her, you feel like the woman could just climb past the shutter and tumble over the windowsill into a hole, to a bottomless unknown, like Persephone, like Alice. Leaning over the sill, she sees the ships we can't. She could jump into a boat and just go. But the morning sail is done. The boats have already dropped anchor and won't leave until tomorrow. In the painting, the sunlight seeps past the shutters, into the spare room, onto the woman. At her feet is a circle of shadow—woman as still, dark pond.

It amazes me now that I lived eighteen years surrounded by those mountains but I couldn't tell you their names or anything about them other than that they were there. When the house on University Circle was new, the housing development was still a tract of dirt and scrub, and I'm pretty sure there were horses there, and a wooden fence to keep the horses inside. My brother used to ride his bicycle in zigzags back and forth along that street between University Circle and the horses, back and forth and around and around the asphalt. I would watch him sometimes, you know, from behind the door through the peephole.

I have another memory of that door. There was a morning I awoke quite early, just before I stopped going to school. The rest of the house was sleeping. I opened the door of my room and walked down the long carpeted hallway and stopped at the front door. I remember the walk to the door taking a long time. Twilight started to show from the room behind me. I put both palms on the door and peered. From this miniature window, I could see my driveway. Beyond the driveway, in the cul-de-sac, was a body. The body moved in a slant; it was limping. And I thought I saw in this loping figure the shape of my neighborhood friend, who had grown up on the cul-de-sac with me, and who had died rather precipitously of leukemia the year before. I pulled my eye away from the door and sat down with my back against it. I stayed that way for a long time until I heard movement coming from my parents' room.

Friends and family said that, in his later years, Caspar David Friedrich became reclusive and odd. He would hardly leave his studio, they said, except to take solitary walks through the woods near his house twice a day, right before sunrise and again as the sun was setting, to no obvious end. One of his only friends, the painter and gynecologist Carl Gustav Carus, described Friedrich as a sharp north German type with a very exalted notion of art and an essentially gloomy nature, and that these qualities, combined with a "profound dissatisfaction" with his art, made it understandable to Carus that Friedrich had once tried to take his own life. The popular story, then and now, was that Friedrich's depression was due to the fact that his paintings had fallen out of favor—more specifically, that they had come to be viewed by nameless "critics" as, to put it nicely, romantic and anachronistic.

Nowadays it's fashionable to disagree with these critics, thus affirming Friedrich's genius, but of course the critics were correct. What else could you call a man who had made it his life's work to follow the sun, who could not stop painting the sun, other than a man estranged from time? You only have to look at *Woman before the Rising Sun*, one of scores of Friedrich's sun paintings, and you will see what I mean. Friedrich painted this woman as if she could be anywhere. Not *anywhere* anywhere—not a city, of course. There is no city in this scene, just a woman standing before the sunrise with an expanse of field in the middle. There are a few trees. There are three boulders. There are mountains on the horizon. Beyond the summit could be a city, a metropolis with crowds pushing, sirens calling, glass and steel shooting into the sky. There could be a wasteland, too, on the other side of the mountains. Friedrich's paintings so often include points of descent. When you were a child, did you ask yourself just where does the sun come from when it climbs up into the sky? But the woman in the painting is uninterested in questions, you can see this in her hands, in the shape of them, how the fingers are cupped and facing the sun, ready to let it warm her palms before sliding through the cracks of her fingers. The left hand, do you see? The index finger pointing furtively down. *This way, sun, this way.* And you can see it in the pose of her forearms, too, outstretched just a bit, upper arms held close. She is still and tall, except for the tilt of her head. The color of the sky is flames. It is nearing the hour of ants, the magic hour. In *Woman before the Rising Sun* there is so much silence. Too much silence. It is painful to see. And painful, too, how the woman is set with her torso right over the sun. The sunshine is shooting out of her heart, out of her ribs and belly,

111

her heart and belly are electrified, but the woman doesn't move. There is a path at her feet, but she does not move. *This way, sun, this way.* Unlike *Rock Arch in the Uttewalder Grund*, in this Friedrich painting, the rocks are guardians. They are sentinels at the woman's side, her companions, her friends. The four of them stand there together, right there with the sun. Friedrich painted the sun so many times, and often in the paintings of Caspar David Friedrich you can't tell whether it is rising or falling. Sunlight moves up and down. But it also moves back and forth, and in and out. Sometimes this painting is called *Woman before the Rising Sun*. But other times it is called *Woman before the Setting Sun*. In *Woman before the Rising Sun*, the rays of the sun are birth, rebirth, renewal. In *Woman before the Setting Sun*, the rays of the sun are death. In *Woman before the Rising Sun (Woman before the Setting Sun)*, morning falls as night ascends. Is the sun coming or going?

I wonder if this is what Friedrich found on his friendless walks, the uncertain distance between the beginning of day and the end, between the beginning and the end. It doesn't matter, in a Friedrich painting, how time passes. Only that time is passing. Like Steichen's Balzac, the woman before the rising/setting sun is a confrontation with the landscape. But unlike Balzac, she is fully there and, unlike the men in other Friedrich paintings, the woman is not small. Yet she is not fully herself either. She is superimposed over the landscape and she is the landscape also. The woman before the rising/setting sun is pointing and radiating and fixed; she is a childless icon. Look again at her feet; she stands at the end of the path, not the start. This woman's abyss is a window too. Friedrich does not paint it, but the window is still there, a transparent wall so easy to break but so hard to move through. It may be that this was how Friedrich felt standing at the edge of a frozen lake at the age of thirteen, as his younger brother drowned before him. The woman herself is at once rising and falling. A woman on her own is a woman. A woman watching the sun is infinity. For Caspar David Friedrich, the sun is a metaphor for the cycle of birth and death. But it is not a metaphor.

Friedrich liked to paint the backs of people: people in nature turned away or, better put I suppose, people turned toward. Both women in these paintings are his wife, Caroline—that's what people have guessed—who, as a rule, is cursorily described in the historical sources as unassuming and young, whose youth and invisibility served as a positive influence on Friedrich's work, if not his personality, and whom I can't help but imagine as little more than a presence moving from room to room while her husband was out in the trees. But every Friedrich painting, even those of Caroline, is a portrait of Friedrich and of us. We, along with Friedrich, are observer and observed. In *Woman before the Rising Sun (Woman before the Setting Sun)*, Friedrich is the woman before the sunrise and the painter before the woman, and we, too, are woman and painter, all of us standing stupefied by what is coming upon the horizon, all of us watched by morning.

So by the time I opened my eyes, the sun would be up and morning would be finished. The cul-de-sac was quiet at this hour—the houses were empty, the residents of University Circle at work or school or elsewhere. Birdsong in the desert is rare at any time of the day. On the other side of Paradise Road, behind the casino walls, metal clattered over the sound of afternoon laughter. Some of my neighbors were there. From the window, I could also see the evergreen trees that had been planted in front of my house when I was one year old. They had become sick and thin, following the rest of the backyard, making it easier for the sun to reach the anguished message my father had scrawled in giant block letters on the driveway earlier that spring.

What were they, the trees? Juniper, I think. They had round pale fruits that tasted like rocks and were the color of a northern sea, the color of water Jules Verne must have sailed across in his little wooden skiff, the color of Jacques Cousteau's eyes when he gazed across the bow, just before diving down deep. Maybe this is the fear we all share: that when the morning comes and shines its light, we will have to read the message that has been put there before us. Or, worse, that there will be so much sunlight and nothing at all to see.

✳

The morning after, I hadn't even been thinking about the ant until I saw the space outside by the tree. The ant was gone, almost as if it had never been there, and the sugar was also gone, and I thought about how the passage from night to morning invites newness but invites absence too.

✳

During the time of morningless mornings, an extraordinary event was happening in the world. The East German authorities, together with the government of the Soviet Union, decided to dismantle the Berlin Wall. I watched the incidents that followed this event as most Americans did, on television, only I watched them in my silent hours, in the recliner, in solitude.

These episodes of the Berlin Wall on television would stay with me all my life, partly because, though I continued to watch them by myself in the house on University Circle in the days and weeks following, I had first seen them with my father one afternoon while visiting him at the asylum, where he had been taken against his will. We were in the visitors' room, where we met a few times a week, and which was set up like a dentist's office, with heavy padded chairs set askew, and fluorescent lights that did not allow shadows, and an island in the room's middle where hospital staff monitored the patients, and a television on one wall. In the places human beings are put when there is nowhere else to put them, a television is perpetually playing. To distract the residents? To entertain them? Maybe television reminds the confined how people who aren't locked up act, how they behave in the regular world, how people on the outside wear hard shoes and go to work. Hospitals have a way of erasing mornings too. It is always bright in a hospital and a television is always flickering. My father and I sat in the heavy chairs as we did every time I came to visit, facing each other, knee to knee. Behind my father, high in a corner between ceiling and wall, I noticed that the television was not running the usual soap operas and game shows. Instead, it played scenes from Berlin: Berliners dancing on their wall, falling off their wall, breaking their wall apart with chisels. Reporters discussed the clips that repeated every few minutes for the benefit of those just tuning in. My father didn't seem to be paying attention to the television but an image inside his head. Around the room, other patients were playing board games or talking to each other. Some whispered to themselves. Next to my father and me was a chessboard. I don't think my father's arms had yet been damaged by his falls, the result of his failing kidneys and eyes. For almost as long as I knew him, my father had suffered from a stretch of unexplained illnesses that intensified as he aged. When I think of my father's arms now, I see them dangling at his sides, though once my father could lie on the ground and balance a chair in one hand.

The floor of this visitors' lounge was covered in loud wall-to-wall carpet, despite the fact of the hospital having been built in the desert. I had seen this pattern of carpet before, lining the floors of casinos, presumably installed with the same fabled purpose: to keep those who dwelled there in a state of blissful confusion. But there were so many rumors about the casinos among us, the children of the city. In fact, we never understood the casinos or their purpose. Mythology is born of incomprehension, I suppose. At some point, my father remembered me and said, *I never thought I would see the day communism would end*. At the time, I didn't quite know what he meant. Whatever was happening on television had significance for my father and the era he had lived through that it did not have for me. My father was a middle-aged man; I was a teenager. For me, the past was still unnecessary and short. The indefinite regress of the time before my birth was not mine but someone else's. Past and present were very much the same, memories so close they were palpable. The relationship between memory and now is not so different from that between the waking moment and dreaming. This is why the story of what happened can never belong to a child. My father, on the other hand, was taking these jumping Germans quite personally. He was connected to them in a way I never could be—not because he was German, but because he was watching his own past unravel. *I never thought I would see the day communism would end*, said my father, half seeing me, and then my father wanted to play chess, which he had been teaching me during my visits and which I would never win.

Ever since that day, I've been fascinated by pictures of East Berlin. More specifically, I'm fascinated by pictures of the morning after construction of the Berlin Wall began, the Sunday morning of August 13, 1961. Waking in the morning is an act of trust. You must believe that when you wake each day, your bed has not traveled to Mars overnight, that the sun has actually risen, that everyone you know has not unexpectedly moved, that there will not be a wall in the middle of your city, that you will not have become a prisoner as you slept, that the sky above has not fallen, that you yourself are real.

You've heard many times about the insidious genius of the snapshot, you've seen it for yourself, how a snapshot stops time, how it captures a moment that is otherwise ephemeral—a moment that is not supposed to last—freezes it, presents the moment for deliberation, calls it to account. Photographs are intended to be visual evidence. But sometimes a photo can have the opposite effect, can make us doubt the frozen moment put before us ever happened. A snapshot, as a rule, contradicts our memories. When it comes to verifying reality, if a snapshot is put up against a memory, memory will lose. We know, though we love it and are continually delighted by its tricks, that a mind just can't be relied upon. I think of the living room wall of my childhood home, for instance—how, gradually, the living in the pictures joined the dead, just like that. I began to wonder, at a certain point, whether any of the people in the pictures had ever been truly alive. Have you noticed how pictures change once a person dies? How the person in the picture becomes both more and less? Photographs, I think, have an incarnational quality.

The Berlin photographs from the morning of Sunday, August 13, 1961 are perfect frozen specimens of incredulity, of that instant when it seems certain that life will go on one way and then abruptly and disobediently does not. Much of the shock was caused by the insistence upon the part of the East German authorities that construction take place overnight as the citizens of Berlin were sleeping. This plan was learned later. The police and the East German army had initiated their work at midnight. Railway lines were cut off, train stations emptied. By Sunday morning, the border with West Berlin had been sealed.

Nearly every photograph of this Sunday morning in Berlin shows the same basic scene. A soldier, a police officer, single or few, armed and standing; and onlookers, single or few, facing them. In the photos where the onlookers are West Berliners, the Wall is in front of the soldiers. In the photos where the onlookers are East Berliners, the people are behind the Wall. But in every photograph, the surprise of the actors is so profound that every face is stone. No reaction, I guess, befitted the tremendous occasion. Both the soldiers constructing the Wall and the citizens of Berlin seem totally perplexed by what is happening in their city. You can see, in the photos, the way disbelief has moved down into the bodies of civilian Berliners, inhabiting them, fixing them to the scene of the crime, so to speak. But it is the soldiers, many just barely men, who seem most amazed by this turn of events they helped to set in motion. Their disbelief is of a different sort from the disbelief of the victims. The disbelief of the victim includes the gift of powerlessness (or presumed powerlessness) and thus inculpability. It is the disbelief of the disengaged. The disbelief of the soldiers is the disbelief of agency, like when you realize that boulder you just pushed off the mountain is now racing to the town below.

What is most obvious in these early photographs of the Berlin Wall is how insubstantial it is. In some photos, the Wall is more of a shelf, standing about waist-high. In others, the Wall is hard to locate; it is merely the suggestion of a wall. In these photographs, the Wall might consist of a coil of barbed wire strewn clumsily along the street with a soldier or two standing nearby. In a photo now held in the collection of the Polizeihistorische Sammlung des Polizeipräsidenten in Berlin, a young officer of the People's Police rests his elbow on what resembles a bus stop, claiming it for the Wall of the future. The officer's thick-rimmed glasses and side cap give him the appearance of a schoolboy. The surrounding apartments, the shops, the roads—the Wall would soon devour them. There's a photograph I've looked at many times, a shot of West Berliners, sixteen of them maybe, standing before a short stretch of rubble about a foot and a half tall. Behind them is the Brandenburg Gate, which had not yet itself become wall. In the tranquil morning hours of August 13, 1961, the streets of Berlin were gouged down the middle, paving stones and asphalt that ran right through the city center torn up and erected into barricades. To build, the East German authorities reminded us, one must first destroy. Suffice it to say, as a barricade, the rubble pile, like the barbed wire tangles, is ridiculous. Any one of the West Berliners could have hopped across the rubble to travel into East Berlin, just as they had before. But the rubble pile stands before them like Kryptonite, has incapacitated the West Berliners. No one speaks in the photographs of that Sunday morning in Berlin; there is only the stillness of shock. Shock, I guess, is the real wall at this precise point in history.

It was nice weather in Berlin the morning of August 13, 1961. How often we think of battles happening in storms or overnight, when so often they happen on a nice morning, when the sky is blue and life is otherwise calm. I've often wondered, whenever I look at photographs of this Sunday morning in Berlin, after living through a morning like this, how waking could ever be the same. A wall is so absolute. You can see a newly built wall and think it's been there forever. The wall between night and morning is just like this too. It is like a storm gate holding memory at bay. Recently, as I was speaking to her on the phone, my mother insisted that she did not tend roses in my childhood yard and had never tended roses. I insisted that she certainly had, and then my mother seemed less sure.

※

Rilke thought that rose petals resembled eyelids and also the lids of coffins. For Rilke, a rosebud was a bundle of sleeping eyelids in anticipation of opening. Who is in charge of the true story of morning? Who holds the key to morning's gate?

sunrise

*H*ow much can be said about morning? you want to know. I suppose as much as how many mornings can be. The only end to thoughts on morning would be the end of morning itself.

So many symbols, but where is the actual morning? Our understanding of morning is built on stories and concepts and songs. But this isn't morning. It is the squares inside the tapestry of morning, the carefully arranged mementos on the too-high shelf of morning.

✳

When I moved to New York City, mornings took on a different color. I wasn't used to city sounds: the radio broadcasts, the early rattle of trucks, the footsteps in other buildings. The night sounds were different too. Across the way, one floor below, an old woman screamed and cursed for hours every evening, sometimes at her husband as he watched TV in his underwear, sometimes standing at the window. My apartment building was one in a series of brick tenements on Powers Street. The buildings were so close together, I could have practically vaulted into the old woman's apartment. I was impressed that no one ever called to complain, to cart this woman away as she furiously pulled her nightgown closer. Of course, they did come to take her away one day, in her nightgown, of course. Not long after, I wondered if she had been allowed to stay as long as she had because we knew she spoke for us all.

I often had trouble sleeping my first years in New York because of the sounds and their implications. My insomnia was a familiar friend. But, after a time, the sounds of the city receded. Or, more to the point, the sounds of New York were there, but part of me had gone off. And one morning, just like that, the trucks and footsteps were gone. It was as if the sheer repetition of nights was its own act of erasure.

In spring of 2010, my husband and I decided, on a whim, to live in Belgium for several months. Once upon a summer night, when walking through Antwerp's old town, I turned down a street that opened up into a square and came upon a street festival that had just finished. I seemed, that summer, to find these Antwerp festivals just after they were over, but that is another story. The square was empty but littered with beer bottles and debris. The food stalls were cleared of food and servers but were in disarray. The scene looked like it had been vacated swiftly and en masse, as though the citizens of Antwerp had been, for unknown reasons, forced to flee their revelry, perhaps to the river, as they had done so many times in centuries past. I wandered through the stalls for a bit, thinking, maybe, that someone might show up to continue the party, but when no one did I headed home for dinner.

You see, I walked through this square almost every day; I had come to rely on the way it was. But that day I had chosen to take another path through the city, and all the while a festival was happening, without me, in my square, without my knowing it was even there. And the next morning, the morning after I had first come to the street festival that had just finished, walking through the square yet again on my way to the market at sunrise, I was disturbed to find the festival had been cleared away. There was not a single stall standing, not a bit of trash to be found. Was this the vision of Rudolf II? The square had reverted to its established mode. I had the disturbing sense then that there had been no festival in the square the previous night, until I remembered it, just like the morning after someone has died.

I understand now what had bothered me most about that evening in the Antwerp square. It was not that the festival had happened without me. It was the unconscious expectation I had, walking through the square each day, that it would never change.

In the summer of 2011, about a year before I moved away from New York—and almost twenty years since I chased two men down Twelfth Street and spent the night weeping over a small bag of words after two police officers had quietly quit my room at the Salvation Army perplexed, not knowing how to console me; almost twenty years since I decided that I was tired of endlessly traveling in my car and would try to make New York City my home—I left my apartment as usual. By that time, I had lived through many mornings. The repetition of mornings comforted me, helped me feel at last that I belonged to the morning, that morning belonged to me. Morning came again and then again: the subdued light entering the bedroom through the bars of an east-facing window; the pigeons on the fire escape; the walk from the bed to the kitchen with the same number of steps; the black tea steeped in an overlarge mug with the name MIROSLAV on the front, a mug I had brought back from Prague the summer I turned twenty-one, my only souvenir, as the books and scraps I acquired there had been wrapped in cardboard and string and sent overseas on a boat, and had gone missing for a year until, one day, the friend I had traveled with called to tell me that she had received a mysterious piece of mail: a rectangle of cardboard covered in Czech postage stamps with my name and address written in black marker.

My morning routine was like a neighbor one sees every day in the stairwell and yet never really knows. Each day I walked the same route from the heavy front door on Powers Street to the corner of Grand Street and Bushwick Avenue, where the subway station was. In New York City, in the morning, the sidewalk swells with the force of human direction. You can think, as many have, that a sidewalk like this is a perverted thing, that people are not meant to be so fast and so close, with hardly a breath between us. How many millennia of effort it took to create that human space, away from the lasting things that don't understand us, that can never understand us; away from the mountains that laugh at our stupid predicament; away from the fathomless sea. But even the buildings that we erected as sanctuaries for our humanity, where we could express our desires and cares, outlast us. Even our houses go on. Over time, however, I came to like the city's collective lack of refuge. I found this stray energy grounding. On a crowded sidewalk in the morning, I let myself be carried along the streets, past the shops and down the subway stairs where, on a train car, seated between two big men with sprawling legs, I would fight the urge to lay my head upon one of the fat men's shoulders.

On this Wednesday morning, however, in August 2011, as I walked the path from Powers Street to the Grand Street station, I saw that a group of people had gathered on Bushwick Avenue. They were sitting in a semicircle on the curb in front of a new construction site. The same public establishments had occupied that parcel of space between my apartment and the subway for as long as I had lived there: a bodega run by a man who had taped a photograph of a field somewhere in Yemen to his cash register; a senior residence I visited every few years when it was time to vote;

a Chinese restaurant whose owners lived in a trailer out back. A Laundromat. A bank. These were my morning places. The people who had collected that Wednesday morning were young and unfamiliar to me. They did not live in this neighborhood—their posture said as much. I remember it being unusually overcast for the last day of August, but this is almost surely my imagination. Beneath the grey sky, a young woman stood before the gathered with a row of orange safety cones behind her. The woman gestured with her hands, pointing to the road, to the passing cars. Some of the others listened to the woman with heads bowed. One man had his head turned toward the sky. There was a police car parked close by, but the policemen stayed inside. Some passersby, locals, glanced back at the gathered as they walked along Bushwick Avenue as usual, on their way toward the train.

The following morning, I walked again through the heavy door on Powers Street to the corner of Bushwick Avenue. The sun was high and bright. Someone had garlanded the safety cones with flowers. Notes and cards were propped around them. This morning, the second, the group was there again but the police car had gone. The people in the group were standing now and were more purposeful than the morning before. A few neighbors slowed that morning as they walked by the safety cones, to better read the cards, but none permitted themselves to stop. Across the street, a woman watched the scene from her third-story window, arms folded over her chest.

By the third morning, the block had turned into a shantytown of remembrance. There were orange safety cones on both sides of Bushwick Avenue now and more flowers and more cards. The street and the pavement were covered with messages that had been scrawled in colored chalk. Candles had been lit. Only two mourners were on Bushwick that morning. I didn't know if the others were coming back. Next to the senior residence was another novelty: a bicycle, painted white and chained to a streetlamp. Someone had wheeled a handful of seniors outside that day, to the front stoop, seeing as the weather was warm.

That night, I searched the news and found a story of a young dancer who had been cycling along the sidewalk a few nights before when her bicycle hit a pile of loose wood. The dancer was knocked off-balance and fell under the wheels of a passing car. The driver of this car was another young woman, but her name had not been given. There was nothing in the story that suggested this young woman knew how her life would unfold that day, how she and a woman would meet, and neither would continue as before.

You may wonder why I am telling you this. You see, with each morning during this week in the late summer of 2011, I found myself increasingly doubting the repetition of morning. The mourners who just appeared one day in my neighborhood had created a rupture. They had created a Berlin Wall. When I put Las Vegas and the cycle of morningless mornings behind me and moved to New York City, I had come to believe, as I had that previous year in the Antwerp square, that the morning could finally be as it was. Just morning. But that is impossible, because nothing really repeats. Again and again we step into the stream of morning, the living, breathing stream. And, in living the morning, we lose it.

I remember the night we sat around the dinner table as the family friend told us how he had washed a dead man's body. He told us how the cleansing did not happen just once; it was repeated several times. Each part of the dead man was intimately washed: the head and the face, the orifices, the insides of the thighs, underneath the fingernails, between the toes, the nape of the neck. The dead man's body was perhaps given an attention it never had in life. Before they washed the dead man, he told us, the members of the burial society washed too, to cleanse themselves, to protect the dead from themselves, to protect them all from the demons. Every part of the vigil was touched by water: pouring, washing, pouring, cleansing, water falling, water spilling. And throughout this they chanted, reiterating the sacred words, and with their repetition sang the stamp of time over the ruthless march of eternity. There is sympathy in the act of washing for the dead. But the dead body is never completely pure, is never completely clean, until it's gone. Until the hour it is placed in the ground, the body exists in suspension. How the living share this experience of suspension with the dead! We are so alive and yet so elsewhere, always crossing thresholds. I remember another thing the family friend said around the table that night, when I had asked him why it was done. *The dead man's body was washed when he was born*, he said, *and now it's washed again*.

I read something by Søren Kierkegaard at one time, in the desert, during one of my endless nights, long before I understood its meaning: *Every morning, I shave off the beard of all my ludicrousness—but it does not help, for the next morning my beard is just as long again*. What Kierkegaard found, while searching for comfort in the past, was that, rather than consolation, repetition creates doubt. We trust the morning blindly until that first morning we wake with fear, the first morning we experience daybreak. Thereafter, we start to imagine all the ways the sky could *not* hold together, imagine viable scenarios in which it falls. Morning is inextricable from what I can only call a fear of starting. You must have felt this too. Once an object is in motion, it's harder to command, as the East German soldiers learned. And yet we must repeat the morning. Repetition is the wall between morning and us—and it is also morning's key. It is the stamp of time on the relentless march of eternity. This is what the tribespeople of Mount Elgon were trying to tell Jung as they woke and spat on their hands. We can't just reiterate the morning. The morning asks us to perform it anew, again and again and again. Every morning comes with the burden of novelty, the promise not just of repetition but of renewal. The morning comes, we don't want to begin, and yet we can't help but hope. That's just the way we are. Morning's doubt is morning's innocence. That is the gift the tribespeople of Mount Elgon were offering the sun, I think. Simply acknowledging the fact of morning repeating, of ourselves repeating, is an act of adoration.

And just as we perform the morning again, we must leave yesterday as we do. Morning is a farewell; this is part of the performance. It is a homecoming, and it is a funeral. Is it any wonder Tsvetaeva railed against sleep? I do not think she was worried that sleeping would be her end. To be sure, from what we can know, Marina Tsvetaeva did not mind dying. I think that she did not want to grieve. Without the morning, in perpetual night, there are no terrible beginnings and so no terrible goodbyes.

Liberate me from the bonds of—day, my friends, she wrote, *understand: I'm nothing but your dream.*

Have you ever asked yourself, as I have, isn't it presumptuous to get up in the morning at all? Pretending to be the first who is trying to live, the first to love, the first to doubt, the first to feel the pressure of making the world go round, the first to notice the light that rises up and over the hill. We shave the beard of our ludicrousness and then it is long again. But every person is so inexplicably, exasperatingly new. How exhausting it is to be born, and how tremendous, the first time and every time. Yesterday, 150,000 people did not live to see this morning. But here I am, seeing the sun again, birds again, body again, again again. The cars rush along the road, the negotiations continue.

Each morning for a week, Bushwick Avenue transformed. Until one morning when no mourners came. By the end of the second week, the chalk had almost faded and was washed away with the next big rain. By the sixteenth morning after the death of the dancer, only the ghost bike remained. Otherwise, Bushwick Avenue was just as it had been sixteen days before. But every morning thereafter, on my way to the train, I found myself waiting for the mourners nonetheless. You see, it's just as Jung tried to say. The morning is not solely ours. We all sleep in a coffin filled with the dirt of our ancestors, on a shared pile of bones.

✦

For a few days now, I've spent my early mornings watching a nuthatch poke its head into the empty birdhouse we nailed to a tree. I've been wondering what the nuthatch is doing. Is it harboring someone in there? I've been thinking it's much too late, or too early, in the season for that. It is winter today—winter mornings are survival. Every so often there is a mass departure into the trees followed by the whistle of mourning doves flapping. A hawk circles, hunting songbirds. I can't see it, but the birds can. They look happy enough from a distance, but that is the deception of windows. When I go outside and look closer, I can see how they have honed themselves. There's no casual snacking in these days of cold like there is in summer days. A titmouse waits in the branches until its turn comes—watching the feeder, watching the ground, watching the sky, watching. Today, after a week of mornings, I realize that the nuthatch has been methodically taking the seeds from the feeder and secreting them in the birdhouse. In the summer, the birdhouse was ignored, our attempts to seduce baby birds a failure. Now it has become a place not for living but for hoarding, the hoarding of morning's bounty. Why should the nuthatch trust that I will fill the birdfeeder for even one more day? All we want is to hold on to the morning.

✦

My father didn't know much about art, though he considered himself an art lover of the first order, and any interest I have in art most certainly came from him. During my first years in New York, I spent many hours in the museums of the city, which are easier to get lost in than the city itself, since museums, by their nature, encourage a certain detachment. I was fascinated by the innumerable things behind glass, so many things numbered and labeled and, in some cases, explained. Where was the hair that held this comb, I would wonder, the hands that held this cup? What had become of the night table on which this relic was placed? Many things appeared older than their labels claimed. In the corner of every room stood a guard. Did she understand that her own personal items were in danger of being one day confined under glass? Or did she know that they were not? In any case, it was in the museums of New York City that I first discovered the paintings of J.M.W. Turner. I will tell you that, despite my father's admiration for art, I can't recall many paintings on the walls of our house, reproductions or otherwise. But toward the end of his life, my father had assembled a small collection of model sailing ships. I found this curious because, as I understood, my father had never been on a sailing ship and did not even know how to drive. On my annual visits from New York, I would sit with my father— he on the couch and I in a chair—in the house he moved into once University Circle had been abandoned by us all. As my father spoke, I would survey his collection. The boats on my father's shelf were classic clippers, as I recall, with lots of masts and sails and wood—explorer's ships of the old sort. I believe he had assembled the collection's first ship himself, during his stay at the asylum. Perhaps this creative act had inspired him to become a collector. Suffice it to say, when I saw the Turner paintings in the New York museums—with their wrecked, leaning bodies spinning in wrathful seas, hanging in the marble halls and former drawing rooms of the distinguished industrialists of the Gilded Age—I saw my father's ships, arranged on a shelf in Las Vegas. I thought, sometimes, I might bring my father a Turner print from one of these museums, to hang beside his boats; I thought maybe he would like that. But for reasons I can't anymore remember, I never did.

My favorite Turner ship painting, one I had seen in a book about Turner I found in the local library after I had discovered his works in the museums, lacks an actual ship. It is called *Light and Colour (Goethe's Theory)—The Morning after the Deluge—*

Moses Writing the Book of Genesis. As I said, there are no boats in this boat painting, but there is a little person in the middle. The person is transparent, hardly there. A mere trace of a man. He is holding a pen, and he is floating. He is almost like a boat. This is Moses writing his book, but it is also Noah and a stand-in for every witness who has survived to the morning after. Below the little person is earth, underwater. Bodies float in the surf. The heads of the drowned are almost submerged too; some heads smile as they sink. I think, though it's hard to tell, that some of the bodies are those of angels. Above the sunken mortals and angels, the writing person sits, suspended in the bubble of morning. There is no more screaming as there was in the night. The waters are receding. The old world is fading back. The new world is anyone's guess.

The deluge Turner refers to is, naturally, the Flood, the biblical Flood that washed away God's first try at civilization. We know now, from the stories that came after this big event, that God had not been so pleased with what had become of his beloved people and that, more to the point, he was horrified. The hearts of God's daughters and sons were filled with evil, we read, and their actions filled with violence. They were corrupt and had corrupted life itself, had corrupted its beasts and birds. Anyone who has ever created something they later found appalling will easily understand God's decision to wipe humanity out. It does not matter what the created thing is—a work of art or a boat or a child—if it is deemed a failure we should like to crush it without haste, blot it out and start over. The failed thing is unbearable to us because it has come from us. When we have known this intolerable shame of debacle, we start to see the tragedy of the Flood as inevitable and why God's disappointment was invariably crueler than his anger. This is what makes the story of the Flood so heartbreaking; it is not a story of anger but despair, despair—as the East German authorities learned in the summer of 1961—that creation must bring destruction, that destruction precedes creation, and that once the Flood was over, and God promised Noah and his sons and every living creature that would tumble from the ark never again to use a deluge against them, and sent a rainbow across the sky to prove it, darkness would forever be inextricable from light.

As his serpentine title makes known, Turner took inspiration from the color theories of Goethe, which the poet had published late in life as an addendum to his verse and quasi-mystical botanical writings. Goethe was proud of his theories. He took no great satisfaction in his poetry, he thought his poetry was okay, that anyway, there were poets out there just as excellent as he, but that in his century—as Goethe told his secretary Johann Peter Eckermann in 1829, not long before he died of heart failure, crying out, apocryphally, in his last breaths, *"Mehr licht!"*—only he, Goethe, knew the truth about colors. I have to tell you, I don't completely understand these color theories of Goethe. But from what I can make out, it seems Goethe, who wrote that *colors are the actions of light, its actions and sufferings,* identified an emotional quality in light that, he thought, was scientifically manifest. Even light strives and suffers.

One day, while flipping through a library book sitting on my fire escape in New York City, I unintentionally put my hand over exactly half of *The Morning after the Deluge,* to keep the pages from blowing around. This act in itself was not very significant. But it was then that I started to see some of what Turner and Goethe saw in the color of the morning sun. Looked at altogether, the light of the sun in the painting appears circular, consummated, as it were. But when the left-hand side of the painting is blocked out, the right side, the deluge side, is dim. Morning light is a smudge; it is much closer to the light of dusk. Dusky light lingers behind the little person's back. At first, I saw this dim light as the light of disappointment, the light of yesterday's grief. And in the left-hand side of *The Morning after the Deluge*, which is so orange, so yellow, so bright, I saw a hopeful sunrise. But the left-hand side is so colorful that the little man can't face it fully. The more vivid the sunlight, the more overwhelming it is to the little cross-legged man. The blazing morning light on the left-hand side of the painting is not an invitation to the figure; light is coming after him, a huge hot blob about to land. Curiously, the more colorful, sunnier left-hand side of the painting is darker than the deluge side.

As Goethe the poet wrote treatises, Turner once wrote a poem. He called it "Fallacies of Hope." "Fallacies of Hope" is not a complete poem; it is a strange collection of poetic fragments, pieces of poems, lines and phrases for a poem that could one day be whole if only the words could learn to rely on each other. Everywhere in "Fallacies of Hope" the word "hope" is repeated. Turner carried this poem with him like a spell. He would often take lines from it and use them as titles or explanations for his paintings, secretly knowing, I believe, that they would mystify his viewers all the more, each line a rage against the gods carrying the same basic charge:

Hope! Hope! Hope!

Lines from "Fallacies of Hope" first surfaced in an 1812 catalog entry for Turner's painting *Snow Storm: Hannibal and his Army*

Crossing the Alps, a beautiful and terrible painting of an avalanche and a descending storm united to swallow the soldiers in their vortex. High in the sky, a ball of sun makes a slight break in the clouds. Turner used parts of "Fallacies" to elucidate *The Morning after the Deluge* too, when he first showed the painting at the Royal Academy in 1843:

> *The ark stood firm on Ararat; th' returning sun*
> *Exhaled earth's humid bubbles, and emulous of light,*
> *Reflected her lost forms, each in prismatic guise*
> *Hope's harbinger, ephemeral as the summer fly*
> *Which rises, flits, expands, and dies.*

In painting *The Morning after the Deluge*, Turner also became a witness. He painted his eyes into the eyes of Noah and Moses, saw the planet as just a bubble exhaled, a bubble of light and color, a summer fly passing through. The reference to flies in Turner's poem moves me most. Poor despised fly. I can see Noah, naked in his tent, away from the animals and the wives and sons, in the center of an obliterated world, with two flies on his arm. The mammals Noah brought with him in the ark would have had months and even years to increase their numbers. They would have walked off the ship and into the broad, peopleless planet, for a rare and short while free. But the flies would have had only days after the Flood to make more flies for the future. They would have stayed nearer the humans too. In the days following the Flood, when the ark had only just stopped sailing, and Noah lay drunk and nude with the wails of Creation still fresh in his ears, the mother fly birthed her eggs, hundreds and hundreds of eggs, to be dropped wherever she could find a place: some garbage, a piece of half-eaten fruit, a carcass washed ashore. A week later, maybe two, the fly and her lover would be dead. How often do we contemplate the first to die, the new world's earliest graves?

For Turner, hope was a summer fly—just like the morning sun. I think, after all, that I was right, that the light on the left side of *The Morning after the Deluge* is a hopeful light. But light is a passing thing. This is what we learned in school by studying the mirage of astronomical objects. By the time the morning light comes, it is already the memory of light. We are forever one step behind morning, stumbling after morning, stumbling after its hope. I think Turner was similar to Friedrich in this. Both artists painted our relationship to the infinite. But where Friedrich painted the natural and the eternal pressed together in an unmerciful and sublime embrace, I see Turner as a painter of impermanence. Colors change. Light comes and light goes. At any moment, the unchanging mountains could crumble, the waters rise and grow silent without us. The light in *The Morning after the Deluge* is the afterglow of apocalypse. It is the light of suffering, and then disappointment, and, finally, destruction. It is the light that might exist if the whole universe capsized and there you were, in the middle, and in place of your human form, a wrecked and aimless boat. Turner painted a companion for *The Morning after the Deluge*. He called it *Shade and Darkness—the Evening of the Deluge*. We are living, simultaneously, in a pre- and post-deluge state, thought Turner. In our minds, if we follow it far enough, time is already over. And it is only just getting started. The evening that moves to flood that moves to morning must return at last to evening and if so, must therefore, one day, move again to flood.

What I didn't notice for a long time was the shape at the center of Turner's painting, dangling before the man. The shape is a snake. But once I saw it—the more I shifted my gaze to adjust the depth of field—the more the human form receded. The man became misplaced and hazy, while the snake pressed itself against the foreground, as though it were pressed against a pane of glass holding the rest of the scene at bay. Perhaps you see this too. I'm uncertain if Turner intended the snake to be shaped like an ankh. I think the snake is supposed to represent the staff of Moses, which was changed into a snake by God when the two met for the first time on Mount Sinai, and which would become a snake any time someone in Exodus doubted God's potential. The ankh is the ancient Egyptian image of life and the eternal that shows up in the hands of nearly every Egyptian deity. The amateur mythologist Thomas Inman once wrote that, when you look at some Egyptian sculptures where the sun's rays terminate in hands, the hands are holding ankhs. This, ultimately, is what J.M.W. Turner painted: people grasping for light, trying to hold on to light, to hold on to hope, to timelessness, and failing. It is well known that the ancient Egyptians worshipped the sun. But isn't worship just an acknowledgment of our limits? Whenever the sun shoots through people, it terminates in hands. *Th' returning sun*, wrote Turner. *Th' returning sun.*

To this day, I can see so clearly the smudgy pastels I found one afternoon in the storage closet next to the laundry room in the house on University Circle. I remember being surprised to see, written in the corners, my father's name. Were they still lifes or ships? I can't recall that either.

*

One visit stands out in my mind. My father and I had played several rounds of chess when he stopped suddenly to tell me a story from my childhood, which my father rarely did. My father wanted to tell me how he tried to introduce me to the concept of infinity. This was when I was about four or five years old. *I would sit you on my lap,* my father said, pulling at the belt of his bathrobe, *and I would ask you, "What is infinity?"* And then I would give him my childish answer, and my father would laugh. I could see that telling me this story pleased him, though it was, admittedly, not much of a tale. Listening to my father speak of his profession was like being handed a pile of random shapes. I think my father was lonely in his work, lonely enough to share it with me. I want to say that the sun was shining in through the bedroom window as my father told me this story, that it made a square of light next to the table where the chessboard had been placed. That my father sat upright in his bed, and that I was in a metal chair next to him. But then again, we could have been in the visitors' lounge that day. I don't think there were windows in that room.

I didn't remember my father ever asking me this question—*What is infinity?* But I did remember a girl in her room, sitting on the floor for hours, caught in a mental hall of mirrors, seeing all of yesterday's mornings in tomorrow's, and all tomorrow's mornings before her. Did my father see her too? He had slept while the television played, and the stars played, and the games of chance continued all night beyond the cinder block fence. My father never told me that, with our game, we were breaking the unspoken agreement between people and universe, asking the forbidden questions, devouring the apple of the tree from which you are not supposed to eat. When he told me this anecdote from his experience of my childhood, years ago from a hospital bed, I realized that my father had identified me as a kindred spirit. I was someone with whom he could share the terrors of the Wolf.

There's a scene, in Bergman's film, where Johan and Alma are invited to the castle of Baron von Merkens, another inhabitant on their remote Swedish island. After dinner has been served, the baron's wife makes an announcement: they will take coffee in the library, where the baron has prepared a puppet show for his guests. As they file into the room, the baron lights the candles at the foot of a miniature stage with care. He claps and asks an invisible hand to turn down the lights. Then the play begins. It is a scene from *The Magic Flute*, when Tamino has been left in a grove outside the gates of the Temple of Wisdom. In the scene, Tamino cries, *O eternal Night! when will you disappear? When will the light find my eyes?* And from inside the temple, the voices whisper back to Tamino, *Soon, soon ... or never.* When the show ends, the guests politely applaud and the baron reappears. *The fatally ill Mozart*, he explains to the guests, *secretly empathizes with these words.* These are words that surface to Johan every night at 3:00 a.m., the cackling voices, the whispers of Judgment: Soon, soon ... or never. There is a thought worse to Johan than the fear he might die at three. The fear that he will not.

✳

Of all the wolf tales I will tell you, *Bisclavaret* is the most true. In Brittany lived a baron who was esteemed by his neighbors and everyone. He was a valiant knight and handsome. His wife, too, was handsome and beloved by the baron. His love was for her, and hers for him. There was only one thing that troubled the baron's wife. For three days out of the week, the baron would vanish. She did not know where he went, nor did anyone in their house.

One day, the wife decided to question the baron. She feared his anger but asked nonetheless. *Long and wearisome are the days without you*, she said. *I wake in the morning sick at heart and don't know why. Tell me*, she begged, *where do you go?*

Wife, replied the baron, *I cannot say. Evil will come if I tell you my secret. If you knew you would stop loving me, and I will be lost indeed.*

But the wife would not take no for an answer. She prayed and pleaded until she wore her husband down. They sat together and he told her this story.

Wife, he said, *for three days of the week, I enter into the trees. There I become Bisclavaret, the werewolf, in the darkest parts of the woods. I remove my clothes and live on roots and prey. I go naked as a beast. But I must not lose my clothes or else I will become a werewolf forever. This is why my lair must stay a secret.*

Husband, cried the wife of the baron, *I love you more than the world. How could you doubt me, how could you hide from me, how could you lose your faith in me?*

And again, wearied by his wife's pleading, the baron told her all.

Within the forest, he said, *just off the path, there is a hidden way. At the end of this secret path is an ancient chapel, where I have wept for myself many times. Near the chapel is a great hollow stone behind a bush. This is the place I take off my clothes and hide them until I come home.*

After hearing her husband's story, the wife thought only of how to get the beast away from her. She couldn't sleep next to her husband and was constantly filled with disgust. Finally she came up with a plan. The wife of the baron wrote a letter to a knight who had loved her for a very long time. *I will give you my heart*, she wrote to the knight, *but you must help me escape*.

The knight came at once and pledged himself, and then she told him all. She showed him the baron's clothes and the hollow stone, and with a kiss, the baron was betrayed.

For one year, many searched the woods for Bisclavaret but none could find him. His family came around wondering where he had gone. And then, around this time, the wife married the knight.

It happened that the forest Bisclavaret roamed was the same forest the king liked to use for his hunting. One day, while out in the woods, the king's dogs began to go wild. They tracked Bisclavaret by his scent and chased him morning to night, until at last they had him cornered. But Bisclavaret found the king among the chaos, and ran to him, and took the king's stirrup in his paws. The king was wary but moved by the display, and called his courtiers over.

Look, he said, *here is an animal who seeks mercy. He understands begging like a man. Let's leave him alone. No more will I hunt today.* At that the king went to leave, but Bisclavaret followed at his side. He followed the king to the castle and there became the king's companion.

So more time passed until one evening when the king was hunting again. When night fell, he decided to sleep at a nearby lodge—as it happens, the home of the erstwhile wife of the werewolf Bisclavaret. When Bisclavaret entered and saw his wife, he became filled with fury. The king and his people were incredulous, as Bisclavaret was so gentle. Unable to be stopped, Bisclavaret lunged at the dame and bit the nose from her face. The men ran to her aid, ready to slice Bisclavaret to bits, but were stopped by a wise counselor of the king.

King, said the counselor, *this wolf has never harmed anyone till now. Let us ask the lady why she is so hated. She was once the wife of a baron who disappeared. Let her tell us why he attacked her.*

And so, bleeding and terrified, the woman who was once the wife of Bisclavaret told the king of her betrayal. Immediately the king demanded that she bring him the baron's clothes and give them to Bisclavaret. In a chamber upstairs, the wolf dressed and became the baron once more. Entering the room, the king kissed his friend a hundred times, and the wife was sent into exile. The true beast in this story, goes the moral, is not the husband but the wife, who in her cowardice and loathing cannot accept her husband's misfortune. The husband prevails by embodying his wolfness, both in nobility and also brutality. The wife, noseless and banished, becomes the monster in her husband's place. And all knew the wife's children thereafter, goes the story, by the lack of noses on their faces. But to my mind, *Bisclavaret* is about waking sick at heart and not understanding why.

✳

After the night my father took the family photographs from the living room wall and put them on the curb, he rarely sat in that room again in the light of day. A blank wall looks okay in the dark; in the dark everything is even and clean. At night, in the dark, the shadows go. At night, people seem to go on forever. When morning comes, we are visible and meager. In the morning, the shadow returns.

A couple of years ago, while doing some research, I came across a short memo, written in one of the journals Bram Stoker kept while he was living in Dublin. In the journal, Stoker had scrawled "Mem for story" and, underneath, two lines: *A man builds up a shadow on a wall bit by bit by adding to substance. Suddenly the shadow becomes alive.*

I don't know if Stoker ever wrote this story or how his idea came to be. But reading this note from his journals made me consider the interaction between shadow and wall. More specifically, between shadow and substance. Sir Isaac Newton wrote that a shadow is just the absence of light. But without light there is no shadow. This is the enigma of shadow. A shadow, like a memory, is both appearance and disappearance.

What makes a human shadow is light trying to push its way through us. We create our shadow by standing in the path of light. Our human bodies are not transparent enough to let light pass in and through us. The human body is so dense, we can't help but block it. We are a wall between ourselves. Still, our substance, our density, is what makes a shadow come to life. As our shadow is not possible without us, we are also the shadow. A shadow is a person balanced between darkness and light.

There is something more to Goethe's theory of colors, something I want to tell you. Goethe's dedication to colors was largely inspired by the optical theories of Newton, which were written one hundred years before Goethe published his *Zur Farbenlehre*, and which Goethe, in his preface to the first edition of 1810, likened to an incongruous and clumsy old castle that had for years repulsed potential invaders through its complex systems of moats and towers and embrasures, and which was held in high esteem only because no challenger had ever broken past its barriers—indeed, had so successfully defended itself that the castle had gone to waste, in the end inhabited only by a few invalids standing ready at the ramparts for the war that had never come to pass. In the years 1786–88, Goethe traveled for the first time to Italy. He had gone to visit artists there, to talk to them about color, which Goethe hoped would inspire his own art. The Italian artists used colors, it goes without saying, but did not, felt Goethe, seem to understand them. In Italy, the mysteries of color became all the more intriguing to Goethe. Once back in Weimar, Goethe continued his studies. He began reading the texts of natural science, which led him to Newton's *Opticks*, a work he hadn't considered since his schooldays.

Like everyone in the world, Goethe would eventually write in his "Author's Confession,"

I was convinced that all colors are contained in light; I had never been told otherwise, and I never had the slightest reason to doubt it, since I was not really that interested in the subject.

This idea he had learned from Newton, that colors were *in* light, that when light disappeared so did color. Yet, as Goethe began to conduct his own experiments with color, spending many days and years watching the seasons, standing at windows, staring at glasses, he began to think that Newton had missed an essential element in his optical work: the human eye. In the "Author's Confession," Goethe tells a curious story about a day in 1791, when a messenger arrived at Goethe's house in order to collect a set of prisms Goethe had borrowed from a friend, the privy councilor Christian Wilhelm Büttner. Goethe had borrowed the prisms in order to further develop his color theories. But time passed and the prisms had sat in his office, neglected. In his confession, Goethe writes how, knowing that the prisms were soon to leave him, he was finally inspired to look through them, which he had not done since he was a boy. Goethe had remembered well the way prisms made colors happen but had forgotten in which way:

I was in a totally white room. As I put the prism before my eyes, I expected, remembering Newton's theory, to see the whole white wall gradually colored, and the light returning from it, broken apart into so many colored lights.

But how great was my astonishment when the white wall, viewed through a prism, remained as white as before. Only in places where it met something dark did a more or less definite color appear.

At last, Goethe looked to the crossbars on the window. In them, he saw "the most vivid colors." Outside, however, *on the light grey sky, not a trace of color could be seen.*

It required little thought before I realized that, in order to produce colors, a border is necessary. At once, and as if by instinct, I spoke aloud to myself: The Newtonian theory was wrong.

As light goes away, so does color. But if darkness goes, the colors go too. No color exists where there is only light. What Goethe saw in his room that day, as grey lingered at the window and the messenger waited outside, was that colors are created in between light and dark. At the place where darkness confronts light, color manifests. And this too: colors are not only the deeds and sufferings of light. They are the moods of light dancing with darkness. Color, you see, is threshold.

In Turner's *The Morning after the Deluge*, that meeting point, that color, is us. The tiny, fragile human sits within the explosion of new color and light. The morning light and color that radiate aren't just some external force pushing on and around him. The light of morning comes from the man too—stripped and still and remote. No longer is the little man able to stand on one side of darkness or light. Darkness and light fill him. He has woken in the morning helpless and exhausted from the torrents and explosions of night, wondering how to try again, to start again. But he already has.

As Stoker's journal note invokes the living, vital qualities of a shadow, we see the shadow not only as the absence of created things, but itself created, wanting to be known, wanting to be seen, an expression of the deeds and sufferings, a manifestation of color. *Our ancestors, forced to live in dark rooms*, wrote Tanizaki, *presently came to discover beauty in shadows, ultimately to guide shadows towards beauty's ends.* You see, my friend, a person is not just a deflection of the light of morning. When light moves through us, and the shadows move through us, we also help make color. We, the living things, the drifters, the shadow makers, are the capacity for morning's color to be.

✦

Sometime in my early New York days, I had the idea to organize my past. At the time the plan seemed sound, as ideas often do. The events of my youth had become confused, a result, perhaps, of my morningless mornings. I had started to believe, in those early New York days, that it had happened without me—my life that is—that I had been asleep the whole time and only now found myself awake, lying in a field with a long beard and toenails, calling for a dog who had long since departed. My plan was to work through a calendar I had purchased for the project while sitting on the fire escape. I chose this work space because it was uncomfortable and high, an iron precipice above the concrete, away from the rooms that possessed me, with their dusty objects I had brought from my childhood home, which had been placed and re-placed in many other rooms before they came to these. I didn't start in order— how could I?—but wrote down events as they came to me, inside a box on the month I thought it might have happened. Days were ignored. But I tried my best to account for the part of the month an important thing had happened—for instance, beginning, middle, or end—and with a corresponding year. I could forgive myself if I had forgotten the exact day or even the month that one of these significant happenings of my past occurred, but often I forgot the year and I found this mortifying. As you can guess, the more furiously I went at this task of trying to catalog my past, the more convoluted it became. It is not easy to put one's life under glass. Eventually, after many hours, I gave the project up. I left the fire escape and returned inside. A wind had started to blow. Below me, I could hear salsa music coming from the private club across the courtyard from my building. I put the calendar in a trunk. It stayed there for years and may still be there now.

Besides painting falling, Bruegel also liked to paint bodies dancing—village revelry and weddings and such. In *The Wedding Dance*, which Bruegel painted roughly around the time he painted *Massacre of the Innocents*, not all the guests are dancing. Look at the upper edges of the painting. Bruegel filled them with bodies turned away. Some are standing in line, but it is not clear what waits at the end. These bodies don't see the dancing bodies in the center of the painting; they are standing but slumped. Some must hold each other up. In the foreground, Bruegel painted the dancers. Men and women leap about; they are focused solely on the dance. But some dancers don't see their partners. Their attention is somewhere else. Their arms reach out and their fingers meet, but their gazes move on by. These dancers look skyward to an unseen presence, mouths parted, eyes wide. One woman allows herself to be kissed, but her eyes, too, are elsewhere.

Dancing is a sort of falling too, and also a forgetting, a forgetting of one's own self. This kind of falling-forgetting can make you more alive, like Alice's fall down the rabbit hole into Wonderland. In these paintings, the dancing paintings, Bruegel shows us that, as falling is a kind of forgetting, it is also a waking up. Just as we can fall asleep, so can we fall awake.

✳

Come to think of it, the family friend never told me how the vigil ends.

✳

How many times I've thought about the days of endless nights. I see myself clearly, more clearly maybe than I can see myself now: The girl on a chair, the television in a dark room. The blank wall above the couch, the cinder block fence in moonlight. The house on a street that mattered, among the billions of people on Earth, to roughly twelve people living side by side. The thrill of experiencing myself in the process of disappearing. I have in my mind a picture of calm, if calmness can be a picture. No, that's not it, not a calmness. A stasis, rather. A torpor.

It seems paradoxical, then, that when I look back to this time, I also see a perpetual going, a girl in a car driving through the desert, walking the desert in circles, land of rocks and scrub. Something about the desert lends itself to circles. It's the urge to find something different, maybe, evidence of change in a place that gives the appearance of being an infinite repetition of itself. In the desert, at first sight, the end looks like the beginning. All things dust and dust and dust. I didn't go to the desert often. The border between city and land was nearly impossible to mark, but you knew when you had crossed it; the transgression made itself known. If I did go to the desert, there was never a time when I didn't believe I would stay in that place for good. But night would fall, and the stars would overwhelm me, and soon enough I was back in the living room chair. Usually, though, I only had to look up and out the sliding glass door to the mountains rising over the cement wall to feel that I was traveling. The mountains out there. From inside and far away, every mountain is formless presence. A mountain far away is a summons. Only up close does a mountain show its shape, and even then only an eyeful at a time.

One evening just before dusk, three years before my encounter with the lynx, when my father was in the hospital again, and I was left in the house on University Circle, I decided to drive to the mountains. In those days, you could drive twenty minutes and be outside the city limits. All that would surround you was sand—sand and an uneasy sense of agoraphobia. To find the mountains, you had to go out farther. Often, if you hit the right spot before nightfall, you might drive past a family of burros. The burros always reminded me of a television public service announcement from my childhood that advertised the animals as available for "adoption" by Las Vegas residents. As a child, I had pictured many times how happy a burro would be in our yard. Yet it never came to pass. This was back in the days, of course, when my mother still tended roses, and the devil's-grass behind the house on University Circle was upright and green. The service announcements never mentioned just how the burros of the valley came to be orphans or what people did with them once they were adopted, though there were rumors of Las Vegas residents displaying the animals in their yards, alongside southwestern pottery and wagon wheels, or using the beasts as pack animals during the occasional mountain hike. This is all to say that the burros were periodically rounded up by the city when their numbers were deemed unmanageable, without a conclusive solution. Several years after morningless mornings had become a habit, I attended a talk at the university. A Paiute man who was living on a reservation at the edge of the city spoke about the burros as by-products of Nevada's mining boom in the late nineteenth century, imported by prospectors as cheap transportation and discarded when the strike went dry. The burros, he had said, were residents of a bygone era who had since lost their purpose, and whose uselessness Las Vegans had come to find intolerable. To this day burros roam the ghost towns of the Mojave, begging for food. They linger on the highways, perhaps waiting for their owners to claim them.

I remember being the only car around as I wound my way up the mountain pass. It was a weekday. Most Las Vegans used the mountains only on weekends, when they would drink at a lodge that had been built in the 1960s, I believe, an attempt at a rustic Swiss chalet of sorts, a bit of European sophistication in the pines, with cabins and a large open fireplace, away from the garish buffets and slot machines, an invitation to walk in the forests or ski when the winter snows came. Of course, there were plenty of opportunities to gamble at the lodge, and visitors had come to expect that their food be served in the traditional buffet style. That day, the resort was locked, presumably due to the season.

I parked my car and grabbed the only thing I had brought with me: a blanket to set on the ground. Details are indistinct, but some stay with me: the smell of pine, the dry surfaces. Just a few paces from the parking lot, I could see only trees and stones. For the first time in my life, I noted how easy it was to just leave, to disappear without anyone noticing. When I was satisfied I was far enough from my car and any possible strays from the city who had come for their own escape, I set my blanket on the dirt and lay down. I wasn't there long, watching the sun fall away from the sky, when I saw a snake coming up over a rock. The snake bent itself around, with its mouth toward its tail. I got up from my blanket and approached the mountain's edge, trying to find the city.

It might be that, in *Woman before the Rising Sun*, there is no invisible wall dividing woman and sun, no wall between woman and landscape. There is only a series of encounters within a circle of time. What we think of as the rupture between sleep and morning, what we experience as a break, is just a person, perhaps, any person, standing before the sun.

some words about the text

My thoughts on the falling of the Berlin Wall were explored in an essay I wrote for *The Smart Set* magazine, which was republished in a collection of my essays (Fallen Bros. Press, 2015).

An earlier version of this book's beginning was published in *New England Review* as "The Hour of the Wolf" (2017).

Many thanks to the website Chronik der Mauer for its work in documenting and sharing the history of the Berlin Wall.

Though "Elgonyi" appears as the name of the indigenous tribe Jung writes of in his memoirs, my understanding is that Ogiek is the correct name.

other sources

Japanese Haiku, Peter Beilenson tr. (Peter Pauper Press, 1955); *The Grey World*, Evelyn Underhill (Heinemann, UK, 1904); *Mythologies*, Roland Barthes (Noonday Press, FSG, 1972; *The Unexpected Universe*, Loren Eiseley (Harvest/Harcourt Brace, 1972); *Natural History*, Pliny; "Nature," RW Emerson (James Munroe & Co., 1836); *The Wonderful History of Peter Schlemihl*, Adelbert von Chamisso (Story Classics, Rodale Press, 1954); *Liquidation*, Imre Kertesz (tr. Tim Wilkinson, Vintage Books, 2004); *Dracula*, Bram Stoker (1897); *The Metamorphosis*, Franz Kafka (1915); *Mystics and Zen Masters*, Thomas Merton (Farrar, Straus and Giroux, 1999); "The Steps of the Commendatore," Alexsandr Blok (*Poets of modern Russia*, Peter France, Cambridge University Press, 1982); *The Lost Journal of Bram Stoker: The Dublin Years* (Biteback Publishing, 2013); *Nine Letters on Landscape Painting, Written in the Years 1815-1824*, Carl Gustav Carus (tr. David Britt, Getty Publications, 2002); *Kierkegaard's Writings, VI, Volume 6: Fear and Trembling/Repetition*, Søren Kierkegaard (Princeton University Press, 1983); "Fallacies of Hope," J.M.W. Turner, found in *Angel in the Sun: Turner's Vision of History*, Gerald Finley (McGill-Queen's University Press, 1999); *French Medieval Romances from the Lays of Marie de France*, Marie de France, (Eugene Mason tr., EP Dutton, 1911); *Theory of Colors*, Johann Wolfgang von Goethe, (Charles Lock Eastlake tr., The M.I.T. Press, 1970); *Goethe's Color Theory*, Johann von Wolfgang Goethe, (Rupprecht Matthaei (Editor), Herb Aach, tr. Van Nostrand Reinhold Company, 1971); *The Immense Journey*, Loren Eiseley (Vintage Books, 1959); *Of Wolves and Men*, Barry Lopez (Charles Scribner's Sons, 1978);); *Fatelessness*, Imre Kertesz (tr. Tim Wilkonson, Vintage Books, 2004); *Memories, Dreams, Reflections*, C.G. Jung, Recorded And Edited By Aniela Jaffé, Translated from the German by Richard and Clara Winston (Vintage Books, 1989).

acknowledgments

Emily Mitchell; Tom Bissell; Michael Stone-Richards; Heather King; Justin E.H. Smith; Carolyn Kuebler, J. M. Tyree, and all at *New England Review*; Bonnie Nadell; Chris Heiser, Olivia Smith, and all at Unnamed Press; Mary Ellen Geist; Jeff Chiplis; Meghan Scanlon; Abbas Raza; Shawn Spencer; Rachel Rafael Neis; Daphna Stroumsa; Morgan Meis.

My mother, my brother, and my father.

Thank you.

about the author

PHOTO CREDIT: MORGAN MEIS

Stefany Anne Golberg has written for *The Washington Post*, *Lapham's Quarterly*, and *New England Review*, and was Critic in Residence at Drexel University in Philadelphia. A multi-media artist, Stefany is a founder of Flux Factory, an arts collective in New York City, and co-author (with Morgan Meis) of *Dead People*, a series of eulogies about cultural icons. Stefany now lives in Detroit where she is creating a museum in her house called The Huckleberry Explorers Club.